Losing Touch with the Living God

Losing Touch
with the
Living God

John Benton

 EVANGELICAL PRESS

EVANGELICAL PRESS
12 Wooler Street, Darlington, Co. Durham, DL1 1RQ, England.

First Published 1985
Second Impression 1990

Bible quotations are taken from the New International Version,
Hodder & Stoughton, 1979

British Library Cataloguing-in Publication Data

Benton, John, *1949-*
    Losing touch with the living God : studies from Malachi. —
    (Welwyn commentary series)
    1. Bible. O.T. Malachi — Criticism, interpretation, etc. 2. Christian
    life
    I. Title II. Bible. O.T. Minor prophets. Malachi. *English. 1985*
    III. Series
    284.4   BV4501.2

ISBN 0 85234 212 8

Typeset by Inset, Chappel, Essex
Printed at the Bath Press, Bath, England.

To the members and friends
of 'Chertsey Street', 1980–1984

Contents

Introduction

There are various periods which become turning-points in the Christian life or in the life of a church. They can be exciting times. They can also be painful times.

I knew very little about the prophecy of Malachi, apart from the fact that it is the last book of the Old Testament, when we as a church began to study it. Yet over those Sunday mornings of the spring of 1982, as we looked at this devastating little book, it seems in retrospect to have marked one of those turning-points. Its serious themes rocked us to our boots.

Somehow the ailments and ills of the church generally, and of our fellowship in particular, were opened up to us. There was a look on the faces of the congregation which registered, 'What on earth is the pastor going to say next?' And sometimes the pastor wondered about that question too! But we knew that God was speaking to us as a little flock. It was a searching time, especially for myself and the other elders of the church, as we were challenged about our commitment and duties as leaders. But it was also an encouraging time. Just as an athlete might feel reinvigorated by the shock of a cold shower, so Malachi hit us and revitalized us. Our faith and love for our Father in heaven were renewed and stimulated. I cannot claim any great erudition for the following chapters, but they did teach us an enduring lesson about being real in our relationship to God.

This is, then, very much a series of practical applicatory sermons on Malachi, rather than a technical commentary. But I trust that the thrust of the prophet's potent message will be unmistakable.

John Benton
Guildford
August 1985

1.
Background information

No one is certain who Malachi was. His name means 'my messenger', an abbreviated form of 'messenger of the Lord'. It is interesting that the word 'messenger' occurs three times in this small book (see 2:7 and 3:1). Malachi certainly was a messenger. No less than forty-seven out of a total of fifty-five verses in his book record in the first person God addressing his people Israel. There is evidence from some early Jewish literature to indicate that the name 'Malachi' may have been a *nom de plume* for Ezra the scribe, who wrote another book of the Old Testament. But we cannot be sure. However, this difficulty of identifying who Malachi was does remind us of one of the first rules of Christ's service. Preachers and Christian communicators are not meant to attract attention to themselves but to their Saviour and his gospel. It is not the man that matters but his message (2 Corinthians 4:5). Malachi is happy to remain anonymous so that people think, not about him, but about what God has to say.

The Jews were God's special nation in Old Testament times. He had chosen them and had made a covenant with them as a nation. God had promised to bless Israel and Israel had promised to be obedient to God. But as we read through the Old Testament story, we quickly find that, although God kept his promises, Israel often broke theirs. Often they were unfaithful to him, turning away into materialism and idolatry. During the sixth century before Christ, because of their sins and stubbornness, God allowed them to be invaded and overcome by the Babylonians. Jerusalem and its magnificent temple for the worship of God were destroyed and the people went into exile in Babylon for seventy years. This was to humble them and to cause them to return to the Lord with all their hearts (Jeremiah 29:10–13).

Malachi's book of prophecy dates from the middle of the next century, the fifth century before Christ. Although the book has no date on it, this is clear for three reasons. Firstly, the book describes a period at which the temple at Jerusalem had already been rebuilt after the Jews had returned from exile in Babylon. Enough time had elapsed since the recommencement of temple worship for the people to have lost their initial enthusiasm for it. Secondly, the book tells us that a Persian governor was ruling the Jews and Jerusalem at the time (1:8). This indicates the post-exilic era. Thirdly, both Nehemiah and Ezra were involved in leading later migrations of Jews back to their homeland and in the reconstruction of Jerusalem during the fifth century B.C. and there is a close correspondence between the situation addressed by Malachi and that found in the books of Ezra and Nehemiah. If you want to check this out, compare for example, Malachi 2:10,11 with Ezra 9:1,2 and Nehemiah 13:1—3,23; then compare Malachi 3:5 with Nehemiah 5: 1—5; then compare Malachi 3:8 with Nehemiah 10:32—39. The failures and sins of God's people which angered Nehemiah and Ezra drew forth the message of Malachi.

The function of all the Old Testament prophets was to call erring Israel back to the covenant and especially to their responsibilities to obey God. They acted very much as the conscience of the nation, reminding a wayward people of their covenant obligations. Thus in Malachi the covenant is a central feature of the book. With this in mind Malachi's prophecy can be viewed as falling into four simple sections:
1:1—5. A statement of the fact of God's covenant love for Israel.
1:6—2:9. The failure of the priesthood to keep their covenant responsibilities.
2:10—3:18. The failure of the people to keep their covenant responsibilities.
4:1—6. A warning of judgement and a plea to keep the covenant.

It will be helpful to bear in mind this outline structure of Malachi's book as we move through the details and applications of the message.

2.
Covenant love

Please read Malachi 1:1—5

The place is Jerusalem. The year is around 450 B.C. About eighty years before, the Jews had returned from captivity in far-away Babylon. Fifty or so years ago, the new temple of God in Jerusalem had been completed. Its architecture and size were not as splendid as was the previous one, built during Israel's economic boom under King Solomon, but it was functional; it served its purpose. On the surface the life of Israel now seemed fairly good and uneventful. There were no major catastrophes. There were no wars on the horizon. True, no one was very rich, but economically they got by. True, the Jews were still under the foreign domination of the Persians (1:8), but at least they were back in the promised land, the temple had been rebuilt and people were getting on with their daily lives. They were settled.

The burden

But there is one man, Malachi the prophet, who amidst this apparent calm is heartbroken and deeply disturbed. If you saw him in the street perhaps sometimes he would look anxious, at other times he would look furious and some- times he would be in tears. He has a weight pressing down on his mind. The word translated 'oracle' in verse 1 comes from a Hebrew root which means 'to bear a burden'. His heart is burdened, loaded down. 'Is it trouble at home, Malachi? Is it trouble at work? Is there another war brewing?' 'No, but it is a message from God.'

God's men are not always happy-go-lucky people. This is not because they have nothing to rejoice over. To be a child of God, to have our sins forgiven, to have God's Holy Spirit in our hearts, to be bound for heaven are glorious things. It is not because they are gloomy and despondent. Christ gives his people peace and joy. It is because sometimes God's men can see the world from God's point of view. The prophet was given a special intuition to see society as God sees it and to feel the situation as God feels it. Looking down on the stubborn, lifeless, bitter religion of Pharisee-ridden Jerusalem, our Lord Jesus Christ *wept* over those sins and those sinners (Matthew 23:37). While the zealous missionary Paul was waiting for friends to meet him in ancient Athens the New Testament tells us that 'He was greatly *distressed* to see that the city was full of idols' (Acts 17:16). Men who are close to God can be sad men. They can be terribly cut up over the sin they see around them. They feel this, not in a sham self-righteous, holier-than-thou way, but because they see that sin is doing the people they love no good. They see sin as a horrible insult to the God they love. Sin is taking many dear people to hell and God is not being loved and glorified as he ought to be. They are distressed.

Malachi is distressed. Malachi is carrying this kind of burden on his heart and it is not the kind of message he enjoys carrying. But he is like an ambassador for God. He must speak this message, which the people may not like, but which they need to hear. He has no option. God has something to say.

In Israel there is a man with God's message. And this message is not for the Persian governor, neither is it for the Egyptians or any of the other surrounding nations; it is 'the word of the Lord to Israel' (1:1). It is a word to God's own people. All is quiet and uneventful. What can it be about? It is not trouble in the family; it is not trouble at work; it is trouble at church, in the temple and the people's worship of God. God has something to say about it.

The book of Malachi addresses itself to a certain kind of

spiritual problem to which long-established evangelical churches and people who have been Christians for quite a long time are particularly susceptible. There have been those long years and they may have begun with great gusto and fervency, parallel to the Jews' return from exile and the rebuilding of the temple. But now time has gone on since that first commitment to Christ and, almost imperceptibly, there has been a steady erosion of living faith and spiritual urgency. The steady round of everyday life, with its stress and temptations, has somehow cooled the spiritual temperature. The adventurous young 'true disciple' has now become a staid pillar of the church. The fiery Christian Union student has got married, settled down and joined the establishment. That committed young nurse never did quite get out to the mission field, as she thought she would.

There is nothing wrong with being settled in a job and a definite geographical location, but somehow the Christian life has become easy. A nonchalant, almost slap-happy approach has crept into our spiritual lives. We have all our theology sewn up and we have become strangely deft at avoiding the crunch-point of those challenging sermons that we occasionally hear. Spiritual flames are flickering low, and for some that seems to be getting very close to cynicism and somehow losing touch with the living God.

Just as with the Jews of Malachi's time, there have been uneventful years with no great troubles to keep us clinging close to God, and our minds have turned from spiritual gain and treasure in heaven to personal comfort. 'We will use our new house for the Lord,' we said. Faith has lost its edge and worship has become formal. Our hearts have gone out of it. We have become indifferent. We have heard it all before. We are indifferent about attending the prayer meeting. And, if the truth were known, we have also become indifferent and negligent concerning our own personal devotions, prayer and Bible reading. We still buy the Bible-reading notes, but they lay mostly unread on the bedside table.

This indifference can become infectious. As we sense the state of one another's spiritual lives in those various little

ways, it somehow spreads throughout a congregation and
the church becomes dead and formal and, dare we say it,
hypocritical.

What is the gist of the book of Malachi? It addresses this
problem of spiritual degeneration, this fossilizing of faith.
It is a book where God's people Israel are in the dock and
God is charging them and accusing them concerning their
spiritual decline.

Throughout the book there is a repeated refrain, a
repeated structure in the Lord's words (1:2; 1:6–8; 3:8
etc). The Lord says, 'You have done this . . .' Then he goes
on to say, 'I know you will claim ignorance and say, "How
have we done that?" But listen, you know what I'm talking
about and it's got to stop!' In speaking like this Malachi
reveals his great awareness of, and sensitivity to, the exact
thoughts and feelings of his contemporaries, which is one
of the marks of a true prophet. He expresses the things
they feel which perhaps they would never say in public.
He exposes that self-deception about our spiritual lives to
which we are all so prone. The pious Jew would never
sarcastically say, 'How has God loved us?' or 'It is vain to
serve God,' in public, while he in fact thinks these things
in his heart. Many is the time that, in spiritual weakness,
waywardness and blindness, Christians have thought like
that, although, of course, they present a different front
as they sit in the pew Sunday by Sunday. God sees all this
and exposes it all in the book of Malachi. He shows why
these attitudes are wrong and have got to stop. Malachi's
book is a call to repentance from lax and hollow religion
and, even more important, it shows the way back to genuine
enduring faith in the Lord who does not change (3:6). It
is the antidote to spiritual degeneration.

The love of God for Israel

These opening verses set before us why this matter of
Israel's formal, lifeless, careless approach to their relationship with God was such a weighty matter. It was such a

terrible thing because it is set against the context of the
fact that *God loved them.* '"I have loved you," says the
Lord' (1:2).

Well over fifteen hundred years before Malachi's time,
God had saved a man called Abraham and made a covenant
with him. God unconditionally promised to bless Abraham
by making him the father of many nations and through
him all the nations of the world would eventually be blessed.
God was going to make Abraham the ancestor of his Messiah,
Jesus, 'the Saviour of the world' (John 4:42). Later, when
one section of Abraham's descendants, whom God had
chosen, had become a large nation, they were in slavery
in Egypt and God used his great power to rescue them,
with Moses leading the Exodus from Egypt. Having
redeemed the nation from that bondage, God made another
covenant, this time with the whole nation of Israel. This
covenant, made at Mount Sinai, laid before the nation a
choice. If they were obedient to him, God would bless them
as a nation. But if in their hearts they turned away from
him and became sinful and disobedient, God would punish
them. However, even in this punishment God had a loving
purpose for the nation as a whole. He would punish them
in order to bring them to repentance, so that they would
turn back to him and he could bless them again
(Deuteronomy 30:1—10). God was determined to bless
them and fulfil his promises to Abraham. God loved this
nation of the Jews in a way he never loved other nations.
He desired to bless this nation in a way other nations had
never been blessed.

What made the insincerity and sinful indifference towards
God of Malachi's contemporaries such a horrible thing was
that God loved them. They were a privileged people. They
were privileged above every other nation upon the face of
the earth. 'I have loved you,' says the Lord.

Maybe we can remember moments in our own childhood
relationship with our parents which will help us to feel the
increased guilt of a crime committed in the context of love.
Here is a poignant poem by Allan Ahlberg about a naughty
little boy reflecting painfully on his antics, with which we
can perhaps identify.

I did a bad thing once.
I took this money from my mother's purse
For bubble gum.
What made it worse,
She bought me some
For being good, while I'd been vice versa,
So to speak — that made it worser.[1]

You can just imagine the little fellow in moments of soli-
tude, blushing with shame at himself, in the light of his
mother's kindness.

As we follow the history of God's promise to Abraham
into the New Testament, we find that, through the coming
of Jesus Christ, the perfect 'Israel', we who through faith
are in Christ have become Abraham's children (Galatians
3:7). We find that the new covenant which Jesus
inaugurated is such that the commitment which God had
towards Old Testament Israel as a nation, he now has
towards Christians as individuals (Romans 8:30). 'I have
loved you,' says the Lord.

What makes it such a weighty and such a terrible matter,
Christian, when, having grown cold and cynical in your
faith, you are robbing God of his rightful praise, is that
God loves *you*. You have grown careless and indifferent
in the context of God's love towards you. 'I have loved
you,' says the Lord.

We live in a cynical age in which the whole idea of the
love of God has been debased. The world looks upon it as
a lot of sloppy, sentimental eyewash. In the churches the
slogan 'God loves you' has often been thrown around with
so little thought that over-familiarity has made it almost
meaningless for many people. This is a master-stroke of the
devil. The Christian message of the love of God is the most
dynamic and soul-satisfying message on earth, yet very often
it is not given a second thought.

It is a tremendous thing to be truly loved by another
human being. Many would give anything to find someone
who really loved them. They feel that they could take all
the knocks and troubles of life which so cripple them now,

if only another person had affection for them. Human love
is a great thing. But how much greater is what is implied in
that statement of verse 2: ' "*I* have loved you", says the
Lord'!

There is a heaven. In heaven God is the centre of all
things. In heaven angels fall down in holy ecstasy before
the Lord, and the awesome musical praise, like the sound
of a mighty ocean, swirls around God's throne. Seated upon
the throne is one who loves *you*. Jesus says, 'The Father
himself loves you because you have loved me and have
believed that I came from God' (John 16:27). Do you
remember the speculation and excitement surrounding the
birth of the baby Prince William to the Prince of Wales
and Princess Diana? What a privilege to be born into the
royal family! What a privilege to be the apple of the next
King of England's eye! What it must be to born into Prince
William's position, with Buckingham Palace as your home,
and the world at your feet! But how unspeakably more
privileged are we to be the apple of God's eye! The King
of love, who walked the earth, whose very garments brought
light and life to those who touched them, God in the flesh,
the best man who ever lived, loves *you*. Christian, the High
King of Heaven, the creator God who speaks a word and a
million worlds spring into existence, loves you. The Lord,
to whom the USA and the USSR are as the dust that a man
might blow off an old book and think nothing of, loves you
personally. You are the one in whom the Lord takes delight.
You are the one over whom the Lord rejoices with singing,
like a young father over his firstborn babe! (Zephaniah
3:17.) It would be understandable if a person became careless
and indifferent towards the cold, distant, aloof 'God' of
Islam. But here is the living and only true God, who loves
you so much that he came from heaven in the person of his
Son Jesus and died specifically for you. The Son of God
loved you and gave himself for you (Galatians 2:20). How
can you have forgotten these things so easily? How can you
have grown cynical and cold towards him? It is all so terrible
because we sin against the love of God. 'I have loved you,'
says the Lord.

But then, you see, having made the great statement of his love towards Israel, the Lord continues. Let us paraphrase verse 2 for a moment. He says, 'I say I love you, but I know how you will respond to that. You would not say it out loud, but I know what is in your heart. You respond with a cynical question: "**How have you loved us?** How have we been privileged?"' So in the rest of verses 2b to verse 5 the Lord brings the evidence into the court room and proves how he has loved Israel.

He points Israel back in their history. 'Look at how I have loved you,' the Lord says, 'with a totally undeserved love.' Others just as good as you I passed by. When the twins Jacob and Esau were born there was nothing to choose between them. In fact your ancestor Jacob was a bit worse, if anything, rather a double-dealing character. But I chose your ancestor Jacob to bless him, while Esau and his descendants, the Edomites, I passed by, so that in comparison to my favour to you, you could say I hated Esau.' The Jews were a privileged people. God loved Jacob and this was no mere irrelevant point of ancient history. As Malachi wrote, God's choice was still having its repercussions in the agricultural and economic conditions of Edom and Israel. 'Look,' says God, 'there's the evidence that I love you. You live in relative comfort, while Edom is a wasteland, the inheritance of the desert jackals' (1:3). '**I have loved Jacob, but Esau I have hated.**'

Christians, too, are the objects of God's loving sovereign choice. The Christian is more privileged than any other person on earth. 'How am I privileged?' perhaps you say. God would point you back to long before the world began and to the doctrine of his covenant love in election. God chose you to be saved before the foundation of the world (Ephesians 1:4–8; John 6:37). God has always loved you.

God would point you back in your own history, perhaps to that meeting where you heard the gospel. There were others in that meeting, just as nice and respectable as you, but, as the Lord opened Lydia's heart to believe (Acts 16: 14), so the Lord opened your heart to trust Christ and be saved, while others he passed by. The Lord loves you. There's the evidence.

Christian young person, perhaps the Lord would turn you
back to the fact that you were raised in a Christian home.
'Worse luck!' you said at the time. But there you had a
mother and father who prayed and prayed for your conversion, while others had no one to pray for them. Your
parents stormed the gates of heaven daily on your behalf,
praying for God's blessing upon your life, so that now you
are a child of God while others have no such privilege. The
Lord loves *you*. There is the evidence.

I was once told by a wise older minister that the overwhelming majority of the spiritual troubles in Christians
are caused by the fact that many are not sure that God loves
them. Having been in the ministry a few years, I believe
that what he said is true. There are many faithful believers
who love their Bibles, who witness for Christ and who have
a measure of love to Jesus, but somehow are not too sure
if he loves them. 'If only I could be absolutely sure that he
loves *me*, then I could face every trial with courage, I would
be at peace and I would be a much more joyful Christian.'
Often, because they feel unable to share this uncertainty
with others, their Christian lives are somewhat blighted. To
such people, Spurgeon gives good advice: 'I once knew a
good woman who was the subject of many doubts, and when
I got to the bottom of her doubt, it was this: she knew she
loved Christ, but she was afraid he did not love her. "Oh!"
I said, "that is a doubt that will never trouble me; never,
by any possibility, because I am sure of this, that the heart
is so corrupt, naturally, that love to God never did get there
without God's putting it there." You may rest quite certain,
that if you love God, it is a fruit, and not a root. It is the
fruit of God's love to you and did not get there by force
of any goodness in you. You may conclude with absolute
certainty that God loves you if you love God.'[2] The Lord
does love you. You are a privileged person.

Here you are with hope in life and a God you can turn
to, while others in the world have nothing like that. The
world to them is as barren and joyless as the wasteland
deserts of Edom (1:3), a place of survival of the fittest
among the world's jackals. Whatever they build and whatever

joy they have will soon be swept away and demolished by
death, while you have a home in heaven (1:4). They are
without hope and without God in the world, while the Lord
loves you.

Israel may not be very well off financially since the return
from captivity in Babylon. But they, who live in 'the holy
land', are to compare themselves with Edom. 'They will
be called the Wicked Land, a people always under the
wrath of the Lord' (1:4). What had Edom done to deserve
this? They had been instrumental in the betrayal of the
Jews into Babylonian hands at the captivity. They had
rejoiced to see God's people in trouble. So God now says
of them, 'They as a nation are under my wrath for ever.
It does not matter what they build; I will tear it down.'
God says that Israel will see this happening (1:5).

Christian, you may not be well off in this world's goods
but consider your non-Christian friends with all their
comforts. They live in the Wicked Land. They are on their
way to hell amid all their luxury. But Christian, you are
saved from the ultimate heartbreak of being shut out of
heaven, because the Lord does love you.

This is what makes this lax, half-hearted approach to
Christianity such a terribly obnoxious thing. God loves
you and you sin against his love and it has got to stop.

The love of God for the non-Christian

But what if you are totally unmoved by this teaching of
God's love to Christians? What if there is not even a glimmer
of a warm response to Jesus who has died? May I carefully
suggest that perhaps it is because somehow you have never
been a Christian at all. In the midst of all the church-going
and the evangelical clichés, you have never actually known
the Lord. You have never surrendered your life to him. You
have never tasted of his loving-kindness. In fact all this talk
of the privileges and special love of God towards Christians
only unsettles you and irritates you.

So let me address you as a non-Christian for a moment.

The non-Christian may say, 'Well, we are not privileged like Christians; you cannot aim this charge of sinning against the love of God at us.' But yes I can! Perhaps not in exactly the same way, but just as really. You too are the recipients of God's love. You too are privileged above others so that you should stop sinning against his love and come to faith in him and be saved. How can this be? Consider two things.

First of all, consider the creation. Consider the universe around us. We live in the days of the programme of the Explorer space rockets. The Russians and the United States send out unmanned, computerized space rockets with all kinds of scientific equipment on board, to fly close to the distant planets, photograph them and find out all they can about them. As the information arrives back from Venus and Saturn and other places, what do they find? They find barren inhospitable landscapes. They find wild desolate places where a man without a space life-support system would not last even a matter of minutes. Yet we look at the earth and we find, not some dreadful science-fiction desert in which man can just about live out a nightmare existence, but, instead, the abundant harvests of the earth, the air and the sunshine, water and all we need for life and health. All the available evidence points to a totally barren universe except for this one place where man lives. This stands as the gigantic evidence that the creator God loves *man*. When God calls you to break with your sins and trust in him, and you turn away, you sin against the great love and privilege God has bestowed on you. The Lord loves you.

Secondly, consider Jesus and what he came to do. You are privileged. God has passed others by, non-Christian, for you. The Bible tells us that not only did man rebel against God and fall into sin, but also an enormous company of angels led by Satan also rebelled and in fact led man into sin. But the fallen angels have been passed by. Jesus did not become an angel in order to save them. He passed them by. He became a human being and through his death on the cross a genuine offer of salvation is made to you. Christ died for our sins and was raised again and *all* who believe will be saved.

God is patient with you, not wanting anyone to perish, but everyone to come to repentance (2 Peter 3:9). He offers you something which he does not offer to Satan and his angels. There is no gospel for them. But to the world of mankind, to you, God has given a promise, and it is this: 'God so loved the world that he gave his only begotten Son, that whoever believes in him shall not perish but have eternal life' (John 3:16). Will you sin against God's love?

3.
Reverence

Please read Malachi 1:6—14

If you were asked to compare your love for the Lord now with the love you had for him when you were first saved, I wonder what would be your honest answer? More? About the same? Or over the years is there now less true heart affection for him? Malachi is accusing Israel and saying that, in spite of God's amazing love to them, their love for God is in dreadful decline. Their hearts are in the deep freeze.

Having first spoken to the nation as a whole, the prophet now boldly turns to address the spiritual leaders of Israel about this vital matter. Much of the responsibility for the sad situation lay with them. In the section 1:6—2:9 Malachi seeks to bring home to the priests of Israel the deficiencies of their service and the influence of this on the rest of the people (1:6, 2:1, 2:7). It is all too easy to criticize leaders and to excuse ourselves and blame them for *our* spiritual carelessness and laziness. But in this case the charge had a definite element of truth in it. Everyone was to blame for the lack of life and vitality in Israel's relationship with God, but fault lay with one group of people in particular — the priests. We will break the section 1:6—2:9 into two parts and look in this and the next chapter at the details of how the priests had led the people astray.

Who were these priests? What were they? Broadly speaking, in Old Testament times, they were a group God had chosen for the special function of mediating between God and the people and bringing them together. Of all the tribes of Israel, the Lord had set apart the tribe of Levi to this task. They were the means whereby Israel could know their

25

God and so experience life and peace (2:4,5). Had sins been committed so that there was need of reconciliation with God? Then God had appointed priests from the tribe of Levi to offer sacrifices for sins, so that a repentant people could be forgiven and fellowship with God could be restored. Did the people need to know how God expected them to live their lives? Then from the tribe of Levi God had raised up Moses to spell out God's laws to them, and the continuing work of teaching and applying the law was still in the hands of the Levites.

Who are the equivalents of the priests today? No one offers sacrifices for sins any more. The one sacrifice of our Lord Jesus Christ on the cross, offered once for all, was totally effectual so that all our needs for forgiveness are met in him (Hebrews 9:25–28). Since the coming of Jesus it is totally illegitimate for anyone to claim to be a priest who offers sacrifices for sins. But a parallel with the Old Testament priests does exist for anyone who through the finished work of Christ would seek to bring God and man together. Are we in a position of spiritual responsibility, seeking to impart the knowledge of God or care for God's people? Then we are in a similar position to the priests. We do not mediate between God and man in the same way that the Levitical priests did. Since the coming of Christ people can go directly to God without the need of a priest. But people can only come to God through a knowledge of the truth. Are we those with a God-given responsibility to make the truth known? Then in this sense we are 'priests'. There is a sense in which all Christians are priests in the work of declaring God's praises (1 Peter 2:9). But missionaries, pastors and elders, as they seek to impart the truth to congregations and be an example to them, are particularly in the 'priests'' position. In Romans 15:16 Paul refers to his evangelistic activity as 'the priestly duty of proclaiming the gospel of God'. Youth leaders, Sunday School teachers and house-group fellowship leaders sit in the same 'priestly' hot seat. The husband and father is the spiritual head of his home and responsibility rests upon him to be a 'priest' for his family. Malachi has a word for all of us in such positions of responsibility among the people of God.

Filled with a sense of their own importance, leaders and teachers can easily become unteachable. There is always a terrible danger that the man who is so accustomed to ministering the Word of God may foolishly become closed to the Word himself and blind to his own sins. To be an effective communicator of God's message to these priests Malachi had first to gain their attention. So he skilfully begins with a statement with which all these 'fathers' and 'masters' in Israel would heartily agree: '**A son honours his father, and a servant his master . . .**' (1:6). It is as if Malachi were about to give a sermon on the subject of how the people should respect and revere those in positions of authority. 'Ah, yes, that's the problem in Israel, if only people would respect the elders . . .' We can imagine all the priests nodding in hearty agreement as Malachi made his first statement. But in so doing, not seeing what was coming, they were walking straight onto the prophet's left hook! Suddenly the whole thing is turned around: ' "**If I am a father, where is the honour due to me? If I am a master, where is the respect due to me?" says the Lord Almighty. "It is you, O priests, who despise my name"** ' (1:7).

Now there is a need to respect *godly* men who lead God's flock by example. But how much more is there a need to respect God himself! The first great factor contributing to the decline of spiritual life and love for God in Israel was a lack of true reverence for God among the leaders of God's people. Perhaps the priests of Israel bemoaned the lack of respect for their position within the community. But at the very same time they were withholding true respect and reverence from God himself.

Reverence has rarely had a good public image. It is so easily given a bad press as being nothing but long-faced hypocrisy. But attitudes to God, especially as we come to him in worship, *are* the true monitor of spirituality. They are the true thermometer of our spiritual temperature. 'The fear of the Lord is the beginning of knowledge' (Proverbs 1:7), and where this is missing we have not even begun to know God. Reverence is not the homage which

weak minds pay to religious tradition and the *status quo*;
it is rather the loving, sincere and practical recognition of
the greatness of God. This was what was missing from the
priests of Israel, with disastrous results not only for themselves but for the nation.

An incident recalled by Jock Andersen points to the kind
of beneficial influence that reverential men of God can have
upon others: 'Professor Victor Rambo, an eye specialist
whose name was well known in many parts of India, had
come to this village to lead the operating team for the first
few days of the clinic. Even in that short period he made
his mark. Many of the villagers had never seen a man of
God before, and he was one. On this particular day he was
expected back from a nearby city to review patients ready
for discharge, and the school quadrangle, surrounded by
classrooms turned into hospital wards, was filled with people.

'Suddenly a large pick-up truck came to a halt in the street
outside amidst a cloud of swirling dust. Out stepped the
professor who quickly attracted a crowd of people eager to
see him and, in some cases, to show him their eyes. He
walked into the quadrangle, greeted his staff and various
local dignitaries, and then followed his usual daily custom.
Looking around at the expectant crowd he called everyone
to join him at the beginning of the day's work in an act
of worship to God. As a hush fell over the place he knelt
down, just where he was in the dust of India, and prayed.
I was interested to note that several Hindu and Sikh boys
knelt down in front of him — such had been the influence
of this man upon them. Amongst the crowd surrounding
him some preferred to stand in the background with heads
bowed. Most stood silently, just staring at this highly unusual
sight of a professor of ophthalmology on his knees.'[3]

This story is a little cameo of the kind of men the priests
of Israel should have been and the kind of serious influence
which their lives should have been having upon the nation.
Instead, catastrophically, the reverse was true. The priests
were irreverent and not taking their job seriously, and if
they were not taking the worship of God seriously, it was
hardly surprising if the ordinary people were not, either.

The symptoms of irreverence

Having charged the priests with failing to honour God and reverence him as he deserves, Malachi pre-empts any protestations of innocence. To paraphrase the end of 1:6 and the beginning of 1:7, he says, 'Are you going to ask how you have dishonoured God? Are you going to ask what is wrong with your worship? Then I will tell you!' In verses 8—14 the prophet proceeds to catalogue a record of their irreverence in worship.

It was painless worship (1:7,8)
The Lord's table in the Old Testament was a table at the gates of the inner court of the temple on which the priests would slaughter the sacrifices. Early in the Old Testament each worshipper would slaughter his own offering (e.g. Leviticus 4:29,30), but by this time the priests had taken over that job. In Malachi's day what was taking place at the Lord's table was the ultimate contradiction in worship. Israel was offering non-sacrificial sacrifices! They were offering to God as sacrifices the things which they did not want themselves. The blind animals, the diseased animals, the crippled animals, the animals the owner was pleased to be rid of — these were the beasts they were offering to God. Sacrifice is the giving up of something we genuinely value in order to express our devotion to God. But the 'sacrificing' of diseased animals was like offering someone as a birthday present the contents of our dustbin! Here was the attitude which presents 'gifts' to God of the fag-ends of our lives. Here was the attitude which says, 'Anything is good enough for God. He ought to think himself lucky I've given him that.' Here was the attitude of 'My career comes first, my leisure comes second and God can have what's left over.' And in practice our attitude towards God often is our attitude towards the local church, which, for all its warts and faults, is the body of Christ.

The point is that the priests who were entrusted with the offering of sacrifices to God should have rejected such sacrifices when the people brought them. The offering of

blind, lame and sick animals was expressly forbidden by the
law of Moses (Leviticus 22:18–25; Deuteronomy 15:21).
But instead the priests went along with the painless 'non-
sacrificial sacrifices'. Either they had such a wrong view of
God that they could not see how offensive and provocative
such things were to the Lord, or they had the attitude of not
wanting to upset the worshippers. 'Let's not cause any
trouble with the congregation; let's not rock the boat – after
all they pay my wages!' God is not pleased when pastors and
elders see sin among the church and are simply prepared to
let it ride.

It was thoughtless worship (1:8,9)
In 'sacrificing' diseased animals they had not even applied
everyday common sense to what they were doing. It was
thoughtless ritual. God makes them face it. Picture the
luxurious dining hall of the Persian governor's palace in
Jerusalem. The governor has had a long tiring day. Now he
has bathed and dressed for dinner and he awaits his evening
meal. The butler enters the state dining room and, uttering
the words 'With the compliments of the chef,' takes the
cover from the silver platter and presents the governor with
a stinking, festering leg of lamb crawling with maggots!
How do you think the governor would react? 'No,' says
God, 'you would be too afraid to bring such a thing to the
governor, so why bring them to me?' Today's parallels are
obvious. God's people who would never dare be late for work
if they could possibly help it are totally unconcerned about
being punctual for the meetings of God's church. Christians
who would never dare fiddle their income tax return make
all kinds of compromises with their consciences over their
giving to God. How can we possibly have less respect for
the King of kings than we do for the political powers who
are appointed by him?
     Verse 9 is ironic. Imagine asking the boss round for a meal
as you are hoping for promotion. Would you give him a
disease-ridden piece of meat? If you did, how do you think
he would respond? Yet you say, '**Implore God to be gracious
to us,**' when you give him exactly the same kind of thing!

Even elementary common sense should have told them that
their worship was totally unacceptable to God and the height
of irreverent carelessness! But no, they were so thoughtless
about their worship that they had not even seen this. 'So
long as we keep going through the Sunday ritual it will be
all right.' Heartless hymns, meaningless prayers, our minds
and affections on everything else but God! Is that how it
is with us?

It was contemptuous worship (1:12,13)
Their worship was defiled, profane and polluted. But,
interestingly, this pollution comes only secondarily from
the substandard quality of the beasts offered for sacrifice.
These sacrifices are polluted in the first instance by the
attitude of mind of the priests making the offering. The
priests are accused of treating God and the things of God
contemptuously. They 'sniff' at him. This seems to be a
colloquialism. We would say they 'turned their nose up'
at God.

What we have here are priests who despise the work God
has given them to do. They find their job a wretched bind.
Here is the pastor who, with his theological college training,
feels that this small congregation in this inner-city church
is beneath him. 'I was cut out for greater things than this,
with my gifts!' Here is the elder who is no longer willing for
the task (1 Peter 5:2). 'What a time-consuming drag to be
an elder!' Here is the man who secretly says, 'How wearisome
being a deacon!' Here is the Christian parent who just cannot
be bothered to pray tenderly with the children. Here is the
Christian who, although he would never say it out loud,
says to himself, 'How dull and tiresome it is to have to give
Sundays to the Lord and get up and gather with God's
people.' Here are leaders who are not just weary *in* the work
(which may well be legitimate), but they are weary *of* the
work. This bored and contemptuous attitude pollutes the
worship. It makes the whole thing into a stench in God's
nostrils. It makes God sick.

It is hypocritical worship (1:14)
Often people cry out to God in prayer when they are in a

fix. Here is a man who, in a time of stress and desperation, not knowing how to save himself, called to the Lord and said, 'O Lord, if you help me now and get me out of this mess, I'll sacrifice to you the very best ram of my flock.' And the Lord *has* helped him, and now the trouble has passed and suddenly the man is saying, 'Oh, well, I'm sure it would have all worked out anyway! I don't really have to give my best because of some foolish promise I made to God during a time of stress. The trouble was not really that bad, but I'll give the Lord this old thing anyway to keep up appearances.' This is pure hypocrisy. It is worship simply to keep up appearances. It is cheating God.

Let us put together the total picture of what God saw in Israel's worship. The sacrifices at the temple came from people who did not really want to give God anything. The animals used for the sacrifices were blemished. They were offered by priests who despised their work and the whole thing was a mindless ritual. No wonder God was in mind to close the temple! (1:10.) Here are the symptoms of hollow, heartless, hypocritical religion. It all adds up to lack of respect and reverence for God.

When God had redeemed the nation from bondage in Egypt he had taken Israel as his 'first-born son' (Exodus 4:22). The Jews had always prided themselves on that father-son relationship they had with God. So no wonder that now God said, 'If I am a father, where is the honour due me?'

The cause of irreverence

Perhaps we gasp at the incredible situation of Malachi's day. We are left asking, 'Well, how on earth had their hearts got this way?' It is imperative for us to know. Perhaps we identify some of Israel's symptoms, present in embryonic form, within ourselves. We fear that such things could easily take a hold upon us. What is the cause of people becoming like that? How do fellowships and churches fall into the barren religion so graphically described by Malachi?

Verses 11 and 14 of our section indicate the cause quite clearly. These priests had forgotten the *greatness* of God. They had forgotten that their God, their 'master', was none other than 'the Lord Almighty', who declares, 'My name will be great among the nations, from the rising to the setting of the sun. In every place incense and pure offerings will be brought to my name, because my name will be great among the nations' (1:11). In response to the hypocrite's sacrifice, the Lord says, 'Cursed is the cheat who has an acceptable male in his flock and vows to give it, but then sacrifices a blemished animal to the Lord. For I am a *great* king . . . and my name is to be feared among the nations' (1:14).

One of the functions which Israel was meant to have, as God's chosen people in the world, was to bear testimony to the truth and greatness of God to the Gentile nations. By their holy living and the blessing that it would bring upon their land, by the awe and wonder and manifest presence of God in their worship, they were to be obviously different from other peoples and so draw the attention of the surrounding nations to the God of Israel (cf. Isaiah 2:2—5). The world would come to reverence the great God of the Jews. But now Israel herself had forgotten the greatness of God.

This is how they had got into this sad spiritual state of irreverence. They no longer realized what their worship was about because they failed to realize the glory of God. They had forgotten that their God was God over all the nations, the sovereign King of the universe. They had forgotten the responsibility they had through their life and worship to cause God to be feared among the nations. They had lost sight of the unspeakable majesty of God and so, subconsciously, they soon took on the attitude that the temple was there primarily for their convenience rather than for God, and the whole sad decline followed naturally. They thought that it was *their* 'church', which existed for their benefit rather than for the praise of the all-glorious God.

This is why, to give them the benefit of the doubt, they asked, 'How have we despised your name? . . . How have we defiled you?' (1:6,7.) They may well have been blind to what they were doing wrong because, having lost sight of the greatness of God, they were no longer looking at worship from the right perspective.

Perhaps our own experience of the majestic greatness of God is so impoverished that we fail to understand its full glory and implications. When Moses had had some dealings with God very soon he found an all-consuming desire springing up within his heart: 'O Lord, please show me your glory!' (Exodus 33:18.) Not long afterwards Moses had an awe-inspiring experience of God as he stood in the cleft of the rock and was allowed to catch a sight of the Lord. 'And he passed in front of Moses proclaiming, "The Lord, the Lord, the compassionate and gracious God, slow to anger, abounding in love and faithfulness, maintaining love to thousands, and forgiving wickedness, rebellion and sin. Yet he does not leave the guilty unpunished . . ." Moses bowed to the ground at once and worshipped' (Exodus 34:6–8). Who can imagine the exhilaration, the joy mixed with trembling which must have been in Moses' heart as he saw something of the glory of God. All we know is that such was the experience that afterwards the face of Moses shone with the brilliant holiness and fulfilment of it all! True reverence is no stranger to joy! No wonder the psalmist expresses the same great passion for a sight of God: 'One thing I ask of the Lord, this is what I seek: that I may dwell in the house of the Lord all the days of my life, to gaze upon the beauty of the Lord and to seek him in his temple' (Psalm 27:4).

David Brainerd was a young American who was one of the early missionaries to the North American Indians. Some words from his diary concerning an experience of the Lord which he had at his conversion may be of help to us here. 'Having been thus endeavouring to pray — though, as I thought, very stupid and senseless — for near half an hour; then, as I was walking in a dark thick grove, unspeakable glory seemed to open to the view and apprehension of my soul. I do not mean any external brightness, for I saw no such thing; nor do I intend any imagination of a body of light, somewhere in the third heavens, or any thing of that nature;

but it was a new inward apprehension or view that I had of God, such as I never had before, nor anything which had the least resemblance of it. I stood still, wondered and admired! I knew that I never had seen before any thing comparable to it for excellency and beauty; it was widely different from all the conceptions that ever I had of God, or things divine. I had no particular apprehension of any one person in the Trinity, either the Father, the Son, or the Holy Ghost; but it appeared to be *Divine Glory*. My soul rejoiced with joy unspeakable, to see such a God, such a glorious Divine Being; and I was inwardly pleased and satisfied that he should be God over all for ever and ever. My soul was so captivated and delighted with the excellency, loveliness, greatness, and other perfections of God, that I was even swallowed up in him; at least to that degree that I had no thought (as I remember) at first, about my own salvation, and scarce reflected that there was such a creature as myself.'[4] Did we realize that our God was that kind of God— so precious, so glorious? There followed in Brainerd a 'hearty disposition to exalt the Lord' and 'to aim at his honour and glory as the King of the universe'.

'Who among the gods is like you, O Lord? Who is like you — majestic in holiness, awesome in glory, working wonders?' (Exodus 15:11). When we realize that in the person of his Son Jesus, this same glorious God became man for us, and went to the death of the cross for our sins, because of his love for us, then we stand with our hands upon our mouths in holy astonishment. How great is our God!

Now the Lord confronts the priests of Malachi's day with their need to recognize his greatness. '**My name will be great among the nations.**' Didn't they realize that the Lord did not need them? He is glorious beyond all telling. It is a privilege for people to be called to engage in his worship. But if people will not worship him in sincerity and truth then God's message is that he would rather that they shut down the church. ' "**Oh, that one of you would shut the temple doors, so that you would not light useless fires on my altar! I am not pleased with you,**" says the

Lord Almighty' (1:10). Would that the deacons put a pad-
lock on the door and the building up for sale, rather than
that this hypocrisy continues! What — and break the long
tradition of worship? Yes! For what is that compared to the
fact that it is hollow, empty 'worship', which brings more
harm to God's reputation than good!

The Lord implies to these Jewish priests that, unless things
change, unless they set their hearts to worship as is fitting, he
will forsake them and raise up other people who will: **'My
name will be great among the nations, from the rising to the
setting of the sun. In every place incense and pure offerings
will be brought to my name, because my name will be great
among the nations.'** Let us take warning. With the coming
of the Spirit in the New Testament age, this is just what God
did. God departed from the hypocrisy of Pharisaical Judaism
and went to the Gentiles, leaving the Jewish religion empty!
Now God can do that with churches. He is not tied to one
church. He is not tied to one denomination or non-
denomination. God is not a Baptist or an Anglican or
Reformed or Charismatic. We must not think that because
we take a certain doctrinal stance therefore God's blessing
must continue. Doctrine is vitally important, but without
love to God it is nothing. God is great. He is not to be toyed
with.

There is a time limit set on all empty worship. God cannot
allow it to go on because hollow religion brings shame upon
his glorious name and his 'name is to be feared among the
nations' (1:14).

Here then is the cause of their irreverence and barrenness.
They had forgotten the greatness of God. They had taken
their eyes off the glory of God. They had forgotten their
privilege of being called to worship him. So their humility
became hypocrisy and their sacrifices as cheap and nasty
as they could get away with.

Conclusions

Let us briefly note four things by way of conclusions from
this section.

1. Reverence is the heartfelt, sincere and practical recognition of the greatness of God. It is the nub of all true spirituality. All spiritual activity will quickly fossilize into empty religion unless this felt knowledge of the greatness of God is alive in our souls. This gives us a way of accurately assessing how worthwhile the various Christian meetings that we attend really are. The question to ask ourselves is not 'Was it traditional?' or 'Was it novel and exciting?' The question to ask is 'Did it give me a felt sense of the majesty and greatness of the Lord and so renew a reverent determination within me to serve him with all my heart?'

2. There is an enormous responsibility resting on the shoulders of spiritual leaders to convey a sense of the greatness of God to the people for whose souls they care. Practical sermons, challenging exhortations, evangelistic messages, warnings against error are all very necessary and all comparatively easy to preach. But a real measure of a preacher is whether he is able to preach from his heart a graphic sermon which lovingly, simply extols God and sends people away thinking, 'How great God is!' No man can do this unless he is personally close to God. No wonder Robert Murray M'Cheyne said, 'My people's greatest need is for my own holiness.'

3. Morbidly dour or legalistic Christians are not to flatter their quirks of character by calling it reverence. Barren silence, sternness and stoicism are not to be equated with reverent awe. We can give a terribly wrong impression by perpetrating such ideas. The French poet Jacques Prevert has a description which could easily apply to such false 'Christian' lives which always makes me shudder. The short poem is entitled 'The Straight and Narrow Road' and its lines in English are as follows:

> At each mile
> each year
> old men with closed faces
> point out the road to children
> with gestures of reinforced concrete.[5]

Truly reverent living is so different from that caricature. It is a profound recognition of the distance that exists between the Creator and the creature, between the holy God and the sinner, mixed with a marvellous knowledge that God loves us. It is that strange mixture of emotions which the psalmist describes when a man 'rejoices with trembling' (Psalm 2:11). It is vital to all true Christianity (Hebrews 12:28).

Satan knows the value of a reverent life and he goes out of his way to wage war on reverence. He tells people that it is hostile to energetic spirituality and is associated with the past and with museum-like church buildings. The easiest way to destroy a valuable doctrine or virtue is to caricature it. This Satan does by suggesting that all reverence is thoughtless homage to the past, it is all hypocrisy, it is all falsely dramatic, it is all insincere. We should therefore desire all the more that the flower of true reverence should bloom in our hearts, so that Satan's lies may be exposed. How we should pray with Moses, 'Now, Lord, show me your glory'!

4. Having seen something of the symptoms of Israel's spiritual decline, how will we know when our hearts are healthy? That is what we should surely be aiming at. We are spiritually healthy when, unlike the Jews of Malachi's day, we have an attitude which believes that *only the best is good enough for our God*. When we honestly offer him, not diseased sacrifices, but the very best of our lives, the best of our hearts, the best of our devotion. That is spiritual health. Perhaps for some of us there is a deep need for a time of rededication as his servants, *to be the best that we can be for him.*

4.
A final warning for leaders

Please read Malachi 2:1—9

George Whitefield, the eighteenth-century evangelist, was only a young man of twenty-three when he first decided to cross the Atlantic. He was to be the military chaplain on the voyage aboard the ship the *Whitaker,* sailing with two other ships to Georgia. Captain Whiting was in charge of the ship and, besides the crew, there were about a hundred soldiers (under a Captain Mackay), twenty or so women and a few children aboard, all bound for the colony in the New World.

Whitefield began to hold public prayers at the commencement of the voyage and declared that he intended 'to know nothing among them save Jesus Christ and him crucified'. The moral tone of the ship was low and his announcement met with nothing but derision and scorn. The officers and crew told him that they believed that his religion was phoney and they would treat him as an impostor. On the first Sunday there was nothing to be seen but gambling and little to be heard except cursing and swearing and the sound of an oboe player entertaining everyone. 'I could do no more', writes Whitefield, 'than while I was writing, now and then turn my head by way of reproof to a lieutenant who swore as though he was born with a swearing constitution. Now and then he would take the hint, return my nod with a "Doctor, I ask your pardon" then to his swearing and cards again.'[6]

Yet Whitefield began to exert an influence for Christ. He visited the sick and shared his provisions with them. He prayed privately for the people. Each morning and evening, undeterred, he continued to read public prayers on the open deck. He took up every opportunity for legitimate socializing and witnessed for Christ whenever he could. Some of his entries in his diary read as follows: 'Had some religious talk with the surgeon, who seems very well disposed'; 'Gained an opportunity, by walking at night on the deck, to talk closely to the chief mate and one of the sergeants, and hope my words were not spoken in vain'; 'About eleven at night, I went and sat down with the sailors in the steerage, and reasoned with them about righteousness, temperance and a judgement to come.'

Gradually, by his evident godliness and courteous but plain speaking, things began to change on the ships. As the journey continued the time came when the captains would come and stand on each side of Whitefield as he preached every morning. Captain Mackay ordered a drum-beat calling the soldiers to these daily services. Often when the weather allowed it all three ships would draw near together and everyone joined in the worship of God!

Here is the kind of influence which God longed to see the priests of Malachi's day exercising upon the nation of Israel. However, with their bored professional clericalism and their contemptuous attitude towards the worship of God, their influence upon the people was negative rather than positive. Their attitude and behaviour caused the people to be cynical about religion rather than to devote themselves to God. But God had the stopwatch on these priests. Time was running out for these people in positions of spiritual leadership. God was about to give them a final warning.

God's warning (2:1)

It is very rare for the spirituality of a group of Christians to exceed that of its leaders. That is a true observation from life which should make all those who aspire to leadership think twice and perhaps tremble. The spirituality of the priests of Israel was at a very low ebb and the effects upon the nation were disastrous. Hence the Lord had a word of rebuke and warning for the priests through his mouthpiece, the prophet Malachi: 'And now this admonition is for you, O priests.'

Leaders should be mature men in the faith. One of the great marks of spiritual maturity is being able to take admonition and rebuke. This matter of being able to own up to your faults and seek to correct them is a mark of maturity in life generally. At one period my wife worked in a school for maladjusted girls in Liverpool. It was quite a place! Although she did not know it at the time, before she was asked to take on the job, all the staff had resigned the previous summer — such was the state of things! There were many incidents, both hilarious and serious, and much prayer was needed to cope with these young ladies. But one of the things which was very noticeable was that these girls were unable to take any form of criticism. If even one sum in their mathematics exercise books was marked wrong, there would be a tantrum. Either the page was later ripped out of the book to try to pretend there had never been any mistake, or in a fit of rage the book was flung out of the classroom window. They were totally unable to handle any adverse comment. They were immature emotionally. This is the kind of thing that happens when a person's self-esteem and emotional security rest upon their achievements and what other people think of them, rather than upon the firm foundation of the fact that God loves them. Our stability as Christians should rest upon the fact that, come what may, we belong to the Lord. A mature Christian leader should have the ability to cope with a rebuke. The way we react to being shown our faults is an indication of how deep and real our relationship with the Lord is.

Now I am not saying this so that every puffed-up Christian will feel at liberty to go around verbally attacking their leaders and pastors at the first available opportunity. Jesus made it very plain that we ought to be extremely careful before we criticize others: 'Do not judge, or you too will be judged. For in the same way you judge others, you will be judged, and with the measure you use, it will be measured to you' (Matthew 7:1,2).

Nor am I saying this so that Christian leaders should become the puppets of every self-appointed, big-headed critic, or slaves to their people's opinions (Galatians 1:10). That would make them men-pleasers rather than servants of God. Yet men are not infallible. They can make grievous mistakes. But at such times mature men of faith will have the discernment to sift the true from the false in the criticism, and the humility to listen and change. To respond well when we hear the voice of God in adverse comment is a sign of a good leader. The apostles were making a mess of the daily distribution of food in the church in Jerusalem because of pressures upon their time and they responded maturely with the appointment of the seven 'deacons' (Acts 6). Peter did not live so as never to put a foot wrong. When Paul had to rebuke him because of his behaviour in the presence of the Judaizers, he responded maturely (Galatians 2).

Paul makes it clear to Timothy that leaders are not to be critized lightly. But he does recognize that the need for criticism and rebuke does occasionally arise and is to be taken seriously: 'Do not entertain an accusation against an elder unless it is brought by two or three witnesses. Those who sin are to be rebuked publicly, so that others may take warning' (1 Timothy 5:19,20).

Congregations can be too quick to criticize leaders and leaders can be too slow to listen. A spirit of love and humility is needed in us all for the right balance that the work of God may progress.

God's judgement (2:2—4)

The priests, who should have been exercising a great influence for good, were leading the people astray by their actions and attitudes. God was very angry with them. He now threatened them with judgement. If they would not listen to his warning then he would move against them in his wrath. **'If you do not listen, and if you do not set your heart to honour my name, says the Lord Almighty, I will send a curse upon you.'**

Note, first of all, that God holds them responsible for their lack of reverence and true worship of him: '**You have not set your heart to honour me.** *You* are to blame. *You* have not done it.' Some people almost blame God for their failure to worship. They say, 'I would love to worship God reverently, but I do not feel moved to; if only my emotions were moved, if only God's Spirit gave me a tremendous thrill and excitement towards God, then I would worship him truly.' While it is true that we need God's Spirit for true worship, it is not possible to blame God for our shallowness or irreverence in worship. Do we feel our own coldness and inadequacy to praise him as we ought? Then we should nevertheless do what we can. Sometimes this is accepted by God as a sign of greater devotion. It is so easy to praise God when we feel on top of the world spiritually. It can be a mark of deepest love when, in spite of the fact that all our emotions are crying out against us and opposing us, we still 'set our hearts to honour his name' (2:2). Do we feel our coldness and our awkwardness? Then we should express this in prayer to God. We should express our regrets and implore the Lord to send us a greater measure of his Spirit.

> Lord it is my chief complaint
> That my love is weak and faint.
> Yet I love thee, and adore,
> Oh, for grace to love thee more!

We can be honest and sincere with God about these things and that is very close to the essence of worship. There is never an excuse for lack of sincerity. But that was the trouble with these priests of Israel. Their worship was a disgrace and they were totally insensitive and even contemptuous about it. *They* were to blame.

How was God going to judge the priests if they would not listen? In two ways.

1. *He would show them up for what they were (2:2)*
He would turn their blessings into curses. It was the great privilege of the priests, after the sacrifices had been offered, to pronounce Aaron's blessing upon the people:

'The Lord bless you
    and keep you;
The Lord make his face shine upon you
    and be gracious to you;
The Lord turn his face towards you
    and give you peace'

                                (Numbers 6:24—26)

Through this the Lord had promised to bless the people
(Numbers 6:27). But now God was going to reverse things
to show up these priests for what they were. Instead of
blessings coming upon the people through their pronounce-
ments there would be a curse. Every time a priest opened
his mouth to bless the people, God would make it mani-
festly obvious that they were not being blessed. He would
make it plain to the people that these men were out of
touch with God, and there is nothing so pitiable as a man
pretending to be a spiritual leader when God has left him.

'**I will spread on your faces the offal from your festival
sacrifices**' (2:3). Paraphrasing for a moment, 'The rubbish
of sacrifice, usually burned outside the sanctuary, I will
spread over your faces.' What does God mean? He means
that he will make visible on the priests' faces the shame of
their crimes against God. What a crushing judgement! They
had shamed God by their contemptuous ways; now God was
going to shame them!

Here are Christian leaders and ministers whose sermons
have become boring waffle under the judgement of God.
'I will turn your blessings into curses.' 'I will turn your
sermons into sedatives!' Here are elders and deacons who
do not lead the flock by example, who are totally ineffectual,
who are held in contempt by the congregation. Here are
Sunday School teachers and 'Christian' parents, and even
the youngsters can see that their faith is just a sham of
double standards and hypocrisy. Here are Christians 'witness-
ing' to the love of God, but totally lacking in joy, and it is
visible upon their faces that they in fact have no vital
relationship with God. Here are 'Christians' who do not
witness at all because it is all just a name.

'I'll show you up for what you are,' says God. 'You cannot go on in this respectable irreverence and coldness towards me and expect to get away with it. I will make you powerless. I will make you a laughing stock.'

What else does God's judgement involve upon these priests?

2. *God would remove them*

The original language of the beginning of verse 3 is ambiguous. It could mean that God was going to make the wives of the priests barren, so that there would be a steady decline in the numbers of the tribe of Levi. Or again it could mean that God would blight the harvests, so that the tithes and offerings which were the main income of the priests would decrease and they would be in want. If they were not offering proper sacrifices to God then, since it was through the people's giving to God that they had their livelihood, God would make sure that their tribe suffered and suffered severely. **'Because of you I will rebuke your descendants.'**

Furthermore, just as the offal of the sacrifices was carried off to the rubbish heap, so the priests would be removed and put on the rubbish heap by God. **'I will spread on your faces the offal from your festival sacrifices and you will be carried off with it.'** Decadent spiritual leaders are fools to think that God will turn a blind eye and allow them to continue. God will get rid of them in one way or another. God will judge them.

There are three brief lessons to note from this section so far.

Firstly, looking at what God was saying to these priests, we must realize that God will judge us for the influence which we exercise upon other people. For the counterfeit Christian, or the counterfeit leader, who has only confirmed the world's prejudice against God's people that 'The church is full of hypocrites', there will be a terrible judgement. Some people start out along the Christian pathway only to turn back because they have honestly been put off by certain people they met in church circles. Jesus says, 'And if anyone causes one of these little ones who believe

in me to sin, it would be better for him to be thrown into
the sea with a large millstone tied around his neck' (Mark
9:42). We are not to think that God's predestinating who
will and who will not be saved makes the person who has
caused others to turn back from Christ any the less culpable.
It does not work like that. Such people will be held responsible. Even the saved must bear in mind that we must all
appear before the judgement seat of Christ (2 Corinthians
5:10).

Secondly, God is a gracious God and his warnings
always have a positive purpose. **'If you do not set your
heart to honour my name . . . I will send a curse . . .'** There
is that conditional 'if', which tells us that as yet for these
priests there is still an opportunity for them to change their
ways, and that is the point of God's warning. The Lord's
desire is that they return. God says that he has sent **'this
admonition so that my covenant with Levi may continue'**
(2:4). There is no record in the Old Testament of God
making a covenant with Levi in the formal sense. But what
Malachi has in mind is the God-given appointment of the
tribe of Levi to the priesthood (Jeremiah 33:21). It was
their sacrifices and their guidance out of God's law which
brought life and peace to the nation as a whole (2:5).

The Bible tells us that God does not delight in judgement.
He delights in being able to be merciful to people. He is
holy, but he is not a belligerent God. God could honestly
say that he desired that these priests should repent and so
he could bless them again and their priesthood would continue. He honestly desired that these men should again
become a holy leadership for the nation. His warnings are
full of love and grace.

Thirdly, if people will not listen to God's warnings then
eventually God steps in and brings judgement. If God has
been speaking to you and disturbing your conscience and
you refuse to listen, and rationalize it away, then eventually
God will judge you — yes, even *you.* Time does run out on
God's stopwatch. He did it with the Levitical priests. Of
course, it was always in God's eternal plan that the Mosaic
ways of animal sacrifice should be replaced as the New

Testament was brought in. But the temporal situation through which that was brought about was the apostasy and barrenness of the Judaism of Jesus' time. God moved in judgement. The Levitical priests were finished. The animal sacrifices stopped. God destroyed the temple at Jerusalem in A.D.70. The tribe of Levi have been replaced by a new priest from the tribe of Judah, even our Lord Jesus Christ. Time does eventually run out. Let us be warned. This sort of thing was not God's way only in Old Testament times. Time can run out for disobedient churches and church leaders! Remember what the risen Lord Jesus said in a letter to the church at Ephesus, sent into a situation so similar to that of Malachi's day: 'You have forsaken your first love. Remember the height from which you have fallen! Repent and do the things you did at first. If you do not repent, I will come to you and remove your lampstand from its place' (Revelation 2:5). And the lampstand was removed! Be warned!

God will judge the professing church for its influence upon the community. Jesus said of the professing church, 'You are the salt of the earth. But if the salt loses its saltiness, how can it be made salty again? It is no longer good for anything, except to be thrown out and trampled by men' (Matthew 5:13).

God's explanation (2:5–9)

In these verses God explains to the priests of Israel how it is that they have lost their saltiness, their influence for good. He explains to the priests why judgement is coming.

The Lord does this by laying before them a comparison of their lives with the lives and attitudes of an earlier generation of Levitical priests. This shows Malachi to be in line with other Old Testament prophets. The general purpose of all the prophets was to call the nation of Israel back to fidelity to the practice and spirit of the things which God had set up in the time of Moses and of the covenant at Sinai.

What were the priests like in Moses' day? After the false start with the golden calf, how did 'Levi' respond when God first gave him the great job of caring for and influencing the nation to walk in fellowship with God?

Attitude

Verse 5 tells us that these early priests responded to God with reverence and stood in awe of him. They had a holy seriousness and deep respect towards the things of God. Their top priority was not that all the congregation should have a bit of fun. They knew they were engaged in business for eternity. They took great care how they behaved, living all their lives under the eye of the holy God. How different all this was from the sardonic, bored attitudes of the present priests!

Teaching

Verse 6 tells us that the earlier generation of priests were careful to be true messengers of the Lord. They were meticulous in their responsibility to preserve what God had taught in the past. They were careful that they did not teach anything false. In other words, although they had an incomplete Bible, nevertheless they knew the Scriptures they had. They made it their responsibility to gain a thorough grasp of God's revelation and knew which parts of God's truth applied in current practical situations. They were not full of their own ideas. They were servants of God's Word, vehicles for its being faithfully conveyed to the people. They were not out simply to tickle people's ears or say the fashionable thing. They could not be bribed into saying what people wanted to hear. They were intent on giving sound principles, right judgements, true guidance at every turn. 'But,' God charges the present generation of priests, 'you have turned from the way and by your teaching have caused many to stumble; you have violated the covenant with Levi . . . so I have caused you to be despised and humiliated before all the people, because you have not followed my ways but have shown partiality in matters of the law' (2:8,9).

Behaviour

It is ever a mark of a false teacher that he does not practise what he preaches. But the Lord is able to commend the earlier priests for the great consistency of their lives. 'He **walked with me in peace and uprightness**' (2:6). One of the things which distinguishes man from the animals is that he is the creature who stands and walks erect and upright. He looks straight ahead. That has significance. It bespeaks the fact that man was originally made for a holy life: not having to look over his shoulder, not having to cower, but with a clear conscience, not having to be afraid of anyone he met because he was upright before God. This is how Levi was in the old days. But now the priests were decadent.

Henry Venn was the vicar of Huddersfield from 1759 to 1771. His life provides a good example of how a combination of attitude, teaching and holy living, such as is commended by God in our verses, does not fail to influence people for good. One incident from his ministry in Huddersfield will suffice.

A Socinian was a person who held the doctrines of the sixteenth-century rationalist Faustus Socinius, who denied the Trinity and that Christ is God. A society chiefly composed of Socinians met in a market town near Huddersfield. These men were full of their own clever philosophical ideas and, thinking themselves intellectually superior, loved to ridicule those who were true to historic Christianity. Having heard of Venn and his preaching, they sent two of their cleverest members over to Huddersfield to listen to Venn, to detect anything in his sermon which they could make fun of and deride, so that they could have a good laugh at their next meeting. So off they went to Huddersfield. But when they entered the church they saw a vast congregation and were amazed at the evident fervency and desire to worship God among them. When Venn went to the reading desk he spoke to his flock as usual with great seriousness, which showed him to be deeply concerned both for the souls of the people and for the glory of God. The subsequent earnestness of his preaching and the devastating appeals he made to the consciences of his hearers deeply impressed the two visitors. One said to the other as they left the church building, 'Surely God is in this place! There is no matter for laughter here!'[7] This man, whose name was James Kershaw, immediately called on Venn, told him who he was and why he had come to church and earnestly asked for Venn's forgiveness and prayers. Without delay he left the Socinians and gave his heart to Christ, remaining one of Henry Venn's closest friends till the day he died. What a mighty influence for good!

To hold God in awe, to give sound biblical teaching and to live a holy life — these are the fundamental prerequisites for spiritual leadership. These basics were missing from Malachi's priestly contemporaries and they did not seem to care. Here is the explanation of why God was going to judge them unless they changed.

God's lesson

From all these considerations, one vital lesson emerges. If we ask the question, 'What is the great work of Christian leadership', what answer does this section of Malachi and, indeed, the rest of the Bible give? Why were the earlier priests so commended? The answer is given in verse 6. They **'turned many from sin'**. The great work, above all other works for spiritual leaders, is to influence people towards God and away from sin.

Spiritual leaders may devote themselves to many praiseworthy causes. It is excellent for people to be brought to a profession of faith in Jesus, but if that confession of love for Christ does not bring forth a changed life of holiness, then it is a worthless profession and the preacher's hopes for that convert are vain. True love for Christ will mean hatred of sin. It is a great thing when people who have fallen out with each other are brought to reconciliation, but if they are reconciled in sin it is worthless in the sight of God. It is marvellous when people are physically or mentally healed through our prayers, but if they are only going to use their restored bodies to carry on in sin it has accomplished little of eternal value. It is tremendous when a congregation feel comforted, assured and secure as Christians, but if they are sloppy about sin, God is not pleased. The great battle in which we are involved is between light and darkness, good and evil, the power of Satan and the power of the holy God.

The true indicator of the success of the church's mission is not the number of people attending services, but the effect the church has upon the moral life of the nation. There must be a *moral* change motivated by honest love for Jesus. Has the tide of sin been turned? That is always an over-riding consideration for spiritual leaders to have at the back of their minds. We are never to lose sight of that.

Therefore shepherds of the flock, elders must not be frightened to talk to people about their sins. We are not appointed simply to keep the peace in the churches. We are appointed that Christ might truly have a godly church which walks the narrow road to heaven. We are to be engaged in doing all we can to turn many from sin. The leadership must speak lovingly and tenderly and caringly, but it must speak firmly on this issue and never let this issue be clouded. Spurgeon makes the seriousness of this matter very plain. 'Remember', he says, 'that Jesus saves us *from* our sins, not *in* our sins. Faith in Jesus does save and will save all who have it, but it is by purging out sin.' Will God be able to write an epitaph of present church leaders, as he did for the earlier priests, that they 'turned many from sin'?

Church folk often do not help either. Should the elders come to speak to us about our lives, we are not to be offended. This is the work God has given them to do for our good. Do not let us hinder them in their duties. They may have to wound us by confronting us with that sin to which we have been clinging, but it is of enormous benefit if we can learn to take such correction. 'The kisses of an enemy may be profuse, but faithful are the wounds of a friend' (Proverbs 27:6).

Blessed indeed is the church whose leaders sincerely command enough respect for this work to be undertaken without hypocrisy and whose members are teachable enough to receive such correction.

5.
How do people lose contact with God?

Please read Malachi 2:10

In Malachi's time, the spiritual condition of Israel was desperately low. There was little heartfelt love for God. There was not much care or fervour for spiritual things. As we have already seen, the lazy, apathetic priests were largely to blame for this atmosphere and the spiritual barren- ness which was dominating the life of Israel. But now Malachi turns his attention away from the priests and focuses more upon the symptoms of spiritual deterioration in the ordinary people.

It seems that some people were coming to Malachi and saying in effect, 'Look, Malachi, we can see that what you are saying about our relationship with God is basically true, but even when we do stir ourselves and fervently call upon God, he will not answer us. Why?' God was no longer answer- ing their prayers. An onlooker could be excused for think- ing that somehow they seemed to have lost contact with God. It is an all too familiar story. 'You flood the Lord's altar with tears. You weep and wail because he no longer pays attention to your offerings or accepts them with pleasure from your hands. You ask "Why?"' (2:13,14.)

'Why is God no longer paying attention to us, Malachi?' In this section Malachi sets out his answer.

The general principle (2:10)

God does not withhold his blessing from people out of mere whim or caprice. When God no longer appears to be listening to our prayers, he does this for a reason. Sometimes it is to teach us patience and persistence and to give us an opportunity to show how much we desire him and his blessing (Luke 18:1–8). More often, however, it is because there is sin in our lives which we are aware of but are unwilling to do anything about. God's answering our prayers does not depend on our being sinless. If this were the case no one would have their prayers answered, for none of us is perfect this side of heaven. However, God's hearing our prayers does depend on our being serious about the fight against sin in our lives. It is not the presence of sin but the *toleration* of sin which shuts down communication with heaven. 'If I had cherished sin in my heart, the Lord would not have listened; but God has surely listened and heard my voice in prayer' (Psalm 66:18).

But what particular sin was so much affecting the communication lines with God in Malachi's day? In analysing the situation of his day the first thing Malachi does is to remind the people of a general principle which runs throughout Scripture.

The book of Malachi began by reminding Israel that their spiritual degeneration had taken place against the background of God's love for them. ' "I have loved you," says the Lord' (1:2). Now, as they come to him with this question about why it is that God does not seem to hear their prayers, Malachi reminds the Jews that God's distinguishing love to their nation had a profound implication. In verse 10 he asks three simple rhetorical questions, the answers to which establish the general principle of which he wishes to remind them.

'Have we not all one Father?' It is unclear here as to whether Malachi is speaking of God as the Father of the nation or of Abraham as their father. But either way the point is the same. The nation of Israel had one father. All the people, great or small, were part of the same family. They were *one* in the sight of God.

'Did not one God create us?' Malachi is probably not thinking of Genesis, but rather of when God created the Jews as a nation at the covenant at Sinai. As people, as a nation, they all had the same origin. They were *one* creation.

Malachi is saying that God has his people in the world (Israel then — the church now), who are bound to him by a special relationship. The implication is that, by virtue of this special relationship with God, they are all bound in a special relationship to each other. They have the same God, the same Father, so they are one, they are a unity. Then comes Malachi's final question in which he draws out the practical inference.

'Why do we profane the covenant of our fathers by break-ing faith with one another?' By breaking faith, by dealing falsely with one another, they were violating the unity of God's people and so violating the covenant which God had made with their forefathers. God's people were being faith-less towards one another. By sinning against each other within the circle of God's people, they were sinning against God. They were tolerating this sin and so God was no longer answering their prayers.

We have a responsibility to be faithful and honest in our dealings with all people, but there is a special duty towards God's people. The late Alan Stibbs pointed out that there is no phrase more frequent in the Bible than the variations of the promise: 'You shall be my people and I will be your God'[8] (e.g. Ezekiel 36:28; Revelation 21:3). In many ways that sentence summarizes God's purpose for the whole of human history. The remarkable story unfolded in the Bible is the story of how God has persevered with that purpose in spite of man's rebellion and fall into sin, and even now he is seeking, finding and gathering a people for himself. Perhaps it is against that background that we best under-stand the seriousness of the sin of needless disunity among God's people through sin against one another. Such sins oppose the very purposes of God.

The general principle which Malachi establishes, then, is that people lose contact with God by dealing treacherously with others of God's people. Wickedly violating the unity of the church will stifle God's blessing.

The New Testament picture of the church as a body

helps us to understand this. If one organ severs itself from
the rest of the body, it dies. If a man loses a finger through
some industrial accident, then, unless something is done
very quickly through the marvels of modern micro-surgery,
the finger dies. Again the church is like an old-fashioned
coal fire. The coal which falls out of the fire very quickly
grows cold. People drift away from God when they no
longer have fellowship with other Christians. Local churches
can go dead through needlessly cutting themselves off from
fellowship with other Christians. Wrong attitudes towards
other true Christians who see things a little differently
from us can dreadfully damage our fellowship with God.
People lose contact with God through sinful attitudes
towards others of God's people.

Dangers for the Christian

If we are truly God's people, Christ has died for us and
all our sins are taken care of by his cross so that we can
never be lost. We are eternally secure. But, nevertheless,
failing to deal with sin properly in our lives, although it
does not affect our eternal security, does affect our day
by day enjoyment of fellowship with God. It is in the context of present felt communion with God that the apostle
John writes those most helpful words in his first epistle:
'If we claim to have fellowship with him yet walk in darkness, we lie and do not live by the truth. But if we walk
in the light, as he is in the light, we have fellowship with
one another, and the blood of Jesus, his Son, purifies us from
every sin. If we claim to be without sin, we deceive ourselves and the truth is not in us. If we confess our sins,
he is faithful and just and will forgive us our sins and purify
us from all unrighteousness' (1 John 1:6—9).

If people are totally unconcerned to fight against sin in
their lives then perhaps they have to ask the most fundamental question: 'Am I a Christian at all?' But even a true
Christian can fail to want to deal with sin properly in the
way the apostle John outlines, and if this is the case he or

she will lose that felt sense of fellowship with God and his or her Christian life will become barren and dry. If Christians tolerate and cover up for their sins instead of coming out into the open with God, cutting the excuses, confessing and repenting, then the knowledge of the Spirit's presence is withdrawn from us, we become powerless in prayer and fruitless in service. That is the price-tag on sin for the Christian!

The particular point which Malachi is making, translated into New Testament terms, is that sinful attitudes and actions against our brothers and sisters in Christ are a very common source of unconfessed, undealt with sin, which shuts down God's blessing.

The New Testament warns us of this repeatedly. After having taught what we call 'the Lord's prayer' in the Sermon on the Mount, our Lord Jesus felt constrained to say to his disciples, 'For if you forgive men when they sin against you, your heavenly Father will also forgive you. But if you do not forgive men their sins, *your Father* will not forgive your sins' (Matthew 6:14,15). While still remaining our Father (we are eternally secure), God will not forgive us if we do not have a forgiving spirit towards others. We will be out of fellowship with him and our prayers will be next to useless.

Or, again, take what the apostle Peter teaches us to be the prerequisite for profiting spiritually from the Word of God. 'Therefore, rid yourselves of all malice and all deceit, hypocrisy, envy, and slander of every kind. Like newborn babies, crave pure spiritual milk, so that by it you may grow up in your salvation, now that you have tasted that the Lord is good' (1 Peter 2:1–3). In order really to get something out of listening to Christian teaching or from reading the Bible, the first thing that must be done is to get your heart right: 'Rid yourselves of all malice and all deceit . . .' And notice how all the things which Peter lists are sins against other people. If we are harbouring jealousy, or slander, or whatever, against others we will lose out; the Bible will dry up for us.

Another example of this principle is given by the apostle

Paul. Notice the context of his often-quoted injunction not to grieve the Holy Spirit: 'Do not let any unwholesome talk come out of your mouths, but only what is helpful for building others up according to their needs, that it may benefit those who listen. And do not grieve the Holy Spirit of God, with whom you were sealed for the day of redemption. Get rid of all bitterness, rage and anger, brawling and slander, along with every form of malice' (Ephesians 4:29–31). The whole injunction is surrounded by warnings not to have a wrong attitude towards others, but rather to be loving and helpful. Nothing so grieves and drives away the Holy Spirit's manifest presence than bitterness against other Christians. Paul's warning is the essence of Malachi's reply to that question about how Israel seemed to have lost contact with God.

Dangers for the churches

Perhaps one of the most dangerous areas today in this matter is the way in which many church leaders and groups of churches judge one another. Much bitterness and barrenness can result from this if we are not careful.

The Bible does make it very clear that all Christians have a responsibility to seek to correct others within the church if we see them going wrong in some way. If there is gross sin which is being tolerated then we are duty bound to go graciously and try to win the folk in question to repentance. The New Testament makes clear the principles of such dealings with others. We are to speak to them lovingly about the matter in the first instance and try to win them back. If they will not listen to us then we are to try again with the greater authority of the wider church circle behind us. If they still refuse to listen, then, sadly, we must cut them off from our fellowship and warn others against them (Matthew 18:15–20; 2 Thessalonians 3:6–14; Titus 3:9–11). In the New Testament the intention behind such actions as these is always that the person should be restored. This is what we long for.

At the present time in the wider church, truth is sadly out of fashion. But the New Testament does call us to be careful about truth. It is good for all churches truly founded upon the biblical gospel to have doctrinal dialogue.[9] We are to recognize that others who are true Christians may in good conscience differ from us in certain areas and we are to have fellowship with them. But when there is a deviation from the Scripture teaching which affects the heart of the gospel and the glory of God there is a necessity to try to do something about it. In the words of T. C. Hammond, we must be careful lest there is 'a surrender of vital principles of Christian belief and practice in a mistaken zeal for unity. We might become like Robinson Crusoe's goats! His enclosure was so large that those inside were as wild as those outside.'

There are some people who are in error simply through ignorance, perhaps because they are young Christians. We need to deal gently and kindly with such folk. But when there are people who should know better teaching false things and refusing to be corrected, then the New Testament makes plain that they should be cut off from fellowship (2 John 10; Jude 12; Galatians 1:8,9). It is essential to do all we can to keep the gospel truth pure. We need to be concerned for the gospel which Christ shed his own blood to establish.

However, when we engage ourselves in this difficult business of correcting another brother it is *essential* that we go about it in the right spirit. Whether it be discipline within a local church, or sorting out differences across denominations or church groupings, it all *must* be done in a spirit of love and humility and of genuinely wanting to see good come to the folk with whom we differ. If that spirit is missing, then it is very likely that soon we will find the Holy Spirit missing in large measure from our gatherings.

1. *We can be too quick to judge others*
There is a famous incident which happened during the Second World War at the prisoner-of-war top security prison at Colditz Castle. Towards the end of 1941 in Colditz the

Nazis tried to persuade the French and Belgian officers to start working for Germany. There was no response on the first day, except much laughter and derisive cheers. On the second day a French aspirant, Paul Durand, stepped smartly forward and said, 'I would like to work for the Germans.' There was a gasp of surprise from the assembled parade and a beam from the German officer.

'You really want to work for the Reich?'

'Yes, I would prefer to work for twenty Germans than for one Frenchman.'

More gasps and looks of astonishment from the prisoners.

'All right, what is your name?'

'My name is Durand, and I wish to make it clearly understood that I would prefer to work for twenty Germans than for one Frenchman.'

'Good! What is your profession?'

'Undertaker!'[10]

Imagine what the rest of the prisoners thought as they saw Durand doing the unexpected. How quickly they could have jumped to conclusions! But how wrong they would have been! Just so we must not be too quick to jump in and condemn other Christians when they embark on something which we would not expect. Some of them may be striking a real blow for God. Perhaps some of them will be acting foolishly, but let us be very sure of our facts and the spirit of our hearts before we begin to criticize.

2. *We can judge others in an attempt to justify ourselves*
Perhaps a new work by some brothers in Christ begins and apparently meets with the kind of success that has eluded us for years. What a great temptation there is immediately to start finding fault with what they are doing simply in order to excuse ourselves! What a temptation there can be to write off anything which is evangelistically successful as 'shallow', rather than perhaps face the possibility that our brothers in Christ may have more faith and more gifts than we have! How egocentric we can be! Now, again, some things will be shallow and based on worldly advertising methods, or whatever. But when that is the case do we find that there

is a genuine sense of sadness in us, or a sense of spiteful glee that we have nailed 'the opposition'? Do we have a loving spirit?

3. *We can enjoy judging others*
Jesus told a most solemn parable: 'Who then is the faithful and wise servant, whom the master has put in charge of the servants in his household to give them their food at the proper time? It will be good for that servant whose master finds him doing so when he returns. I tell you the truth, he will put him in charge of all his possessions. But suppose that servant is wicked and says to himself, "My master is staying away a long time,"'and *he then begins to beat his fellow servants* and to eat and drink with drunkards. The master of that servant will come on a day when he does not expect him and at an hour he is not aware of. He will cut him to pieces and assign him a place with the hypocrites, where there will be weeping and gnashing of teeth' (Matthew 24:45–51). The way I read this parable is that the servants spoken of initially are church leaders, 'in charge of the servants in the household to give them their food'. Jesus points out that there is more than one way in which such a leader can turn out to be an unsaved hypocrite. There is the secret immoral life, 'eating and drinking with the drunkards'. But there is also in this foolish servant a seemingly vicious delight in beating his fellow servants. It is hardly likely that the Lord was thinking of a man who physically attacks his congregation or other servants. It is far more likely that he means some bigoted pulpiteer whose greatest delight is to tell everyone where this brother and that brother are wrong for the flimsiest of reasons. Yes, we do need to seek to correct one another, but, oh, how careful we must be about how we go about it!

Paul writes, 'Brothers, if someone is caught in a sin, you who are spiritual should restore him gently. But watch yourself, or you also may be tempted' (Galatians 6:1). We can be tempted to fall into the same sin that we are seeking to recover our brother from, but there is also the much more subtle temptation of pride and lording it over others.

Jesus said, 'In the same way you judge others, you will
be judged, and with the measure you use, it will be measured
to you' (Matthew 7:2). How do people run into barrenness
and lose contact with God? One way is that if we are harshly
criticizing and withdrawing our fellowship from others, we
may well find God withdrawing his fellowship from us.

'Have we not all one Father? Did not one God create
us? Why do we profane the covenant of our fathers by
breaking faith with one another?'

6.
Intermarriage

Please read Malachi 2:11,12

We have seen that Malachi has laid down a general principle that people can lose contact with God through sinning against the unity of God's people. In verses 11 and 12 of chapter 2 we have Malachi's first application of this general principle. In what ways in particular were the Jews of Malachi's day sinning, so that God would not listen to their prayers? The prophet's answer was **'By marrying the daughter of a foreign God'** (2:11). The unity of God's people was violated and the Lord displeased by the practice of some Jews marrying outside God's people. They were being faithless to one another.

We should say straight away that the command to Old Testament Israel not to marry outside the people of God was *not* an objection to intermarriage with other nations based on racial grounds. Back in the time of the Exodus, for example, people of other nations had left Egypt with the Israelites (Exodus 12:38) but because those people submitted to Israel's religion, intermarriage with them had become possible. Again in Israel's past, Boaz had married Ruth the Moabitess. She was of a different nation, but the point was that she had forsaken the gods of her country and committed herself to the God of Israel (Ruth 1:16). She in fact became one of the ancestors of the Lord Jesus Christ (Matthew 1:5). The grounds for God's objecting to marriage outside God's people were religious, not racial. He expressly forbad any Jew to marry someone who worshipped the false gods of other nations. Verse 11 puts the finger right on the problem. Some Jews of Malachi's day were marrying not just foreigners, but 'the daughters of a foreign god'. To call someone a 'daughter' of a god meant that that woman still worshipped the false god; she was still one spiritually with an idol. So it is on spiritual grounds, not racial grounds, that Malachi accuses the people of Israel of 'profaning the covenant of our fathers and breaking faith with one another' (2:10).

Moses' law made it perfectly clear to the Old Testament Jews that God did not want them to marry outside God's people. 'When the Lord your God brings you into the land you are entering to possess and drives out before you many nations — the Hittites, Girgashites, Amorites, Canaanites, Perizzites, Hivites and Jebusites . . . Do not intermarry with them. Do not give your daughters to their sons or take their daughters for your sons, for they will turn your sons away from following me to serve other gods, and the Lord's anger will burn against you and quickly destroy you' (Deuteronomy 7:1–4).

A similar injunction comes to us as a totally spiritual command in the New Testament. For example, Paul writes to the Christians in Corinth: 'A woman is bound to her husband as long as he lives. But if her husband dies, she is free to marry anyone she wishes, *but he must belong to the Lord*' (1 Corinthians 7:39). Again he writes, 'Do not be yoked together with unbelievers. For what do righteousness and wickedness have in common? Or what fellowship can light have with darkness?' (2 Corinthians 6:14.) A Christian must not marry a non-Christian. A Christian must only marry a Christian.

One of the great reasons that Malachi's contemporaries were in such a low spiritual state was because they had ignored God's command not to marry outside God's people.

How serious is this sin?

We should note the strong language which God uses to describe what the Jews have done in choosing a marriage partner from outside the circle of the people of God.

*It is to 'break faith' and to 'deal treacherously' with God's
people (2:10)*
'How can that be?' you may say. 'The person I marry is my
own affair; it has nothing to do with other Christians. I'm
not hurting them.'

But that is not the case. To marry outside the people of
God is to deal treacherously with your brothers and sisters.
How?

When you became a Christian you joined the body of
Christ. We are committed to each other. Ultimately, just
like the Old Testament Jews, we have no other friends in
the world, except each other. We are called to love one
another, to work together, to bleed together, to cry together!
'Yes,' you say. But now, in saying that marriage is your
own private affair, you are saying something different.

When you joined the church, you committed yourself
to God's people, for whom the worship of God and sub-
mission to his Word in Scripture is of utmost importance.
'Yes,' you say, 'I am one with you in that.' But now, in
wanting to marry outside the Christian family, you are saying something different. You are saying two different things
at the same time. Your words say one thing and your actions
are saying completely the opposite. You are dealing
treacherously with God's people. Your action is a great
discouragement to God's people.

You say that you are committed to work with God's
people for the glory of God and all your life is based on
that. But you do not consider that whom you marry will
either strengthen or weaken the church. If you marry a
Christian, you can both put your energies to God's work.
But if you marry a non-Christian, although you may continue to attend church, which is ultimately doubtful, you
will forever be torn in two directions — to work for the
kingdom or to please your marriage partner. Whom you
marry decides whether or not you will be a worker or a
passenger, a helper or one always in need of help.

*It is a 'detestable thing' which 'desecrates the sanctuary the
Lord loves' (2:11)*
These are very serious words. How can it be that marrying

a non-Christian is desecrating God's sanctuary, an act comparable with blasphemy? Let me suggest a few lines of thought.

1. The sanctuary which the Lord loves is your heart. He is to be pre-eminent there. He is to sit on the throne there. He is to rule there. That is what the heart of man was made for. Now, God, who is our gracious Creator and Redeemer and who knows us better than we know ourselves, has made it very clear that he does not want us to marry outside the family of his people. He has said this for his own glory and for our good. 'Do not give your heart to one who does not love me! Do not give your heart to a marriage partner who has no regard for Jesus, who died for you!' But you say, 'Yes, I will!' The apostle Paul writes, 'If anyone does not love the Lord — a curse be on him' (1 Corinthians 16: 22.) But you say, 'Let me marry him!'

2. It is described as such a serious sin, 'a detestable thing', because the person who deliberately and knowingly goes against the Word of God and marries a non-Christian could not care less about his or her personal witness for Christ. You will set up a home together, but it will not be the kind of home which can be used in hospitality to share the gospel with others. There will always be an obstacle. Again, the person who marries a non-Christian could not care less about the atmosphere in which any children of the marriage might be brought up. At best from the non-Christian partner the children will get only the impression of cool indifference to the things of God. At worst they will find blatant opposition. How will that help them to see the claims of God upon them? Non-Christians can be the most charming and kind of people, but with the best will towards them in the world, they do not love Christ.

3. Why is this ignoring of God's command to marry within the Christian community 'a detestable thing' which 'desecrates God's sanctuary'? Perhaps for some people we need to go right to the root and see something terrible in the eyes of God. If you are asked, 'Why do you want to marry that non-Christian? What is it about him that you love?' For *some* the answer to that question may well be this: what

you love about that non-Christian man, church-going girl, is the aggressive, crude, macho masculinity! What you love about that non-Christian girl, church-going young man, is her tawdry, brazen sexuality! What you love about them is their *ungodliness,* and your attachment to that person only betrays the true desires of your own heart, covered with a flimsy film of church attendance! A detestable thing is there in the sanctuary of your heart. It is desecrated by these things and rather than seeking to struggle against them you are committing yourself to feed those desires. Can you see how serious this is?

4. It is a detestable thing because, by marrying a non-Christian, you are giving your marriage partner the impression that the commands of God do not really matter too much. You are aiding him or her in ignoring the things of God. You are doing him or her spiritual harm. God is not pleased because of the damage you may well be doing to him or her. Consider the spiritual welfare of the non-Christian!

The person who does this deliberately provokes God to say, 'May the Lord cut him off' (2:12)

Whoever the person may be, great or small, rich or poor, old or young, 'May the Lord cut him off from the tents of Jacob — even though he brings offerings to the Lord Almighty.'

In the Old Testament, the idea of a person being 'cut off' means that that person is denied access to God's people and thus to the presence of God, whose sanctuary was in the midst of his people.

How serious is this sin? In the last analysis these verses connect marriage outside God's family with the possibility of apostasy and being lost. Do not be deceived, remember Christ's parable of the sower. He speaks of some seed which springs up and looks good but then, like seed sown among thorns which is eventually strangled to death, 'the worries of this life, the deceitfulness of riches and the desires for other things come in and choke the word, making it unfruitful' (Mark 4:19). There are some people who appear to start the Christian life well, but in fact were never saved at all, and at some point along the way they come to feel that the claims of Christ are just too tough for them and they turn back into the world never to return to him. Such people are lost (Hebrews 6:4—6). How can you tell the difference between a Christian who has backslidden and one of these lost apostate people? The difference is that the person who really is a Christian who has just backslidden will eventually return to Christ; the apostate never does. Now for many people, especially young people, this matter of Christ's lordship over whom we are to marry is the crunch. They go against the Word of God in this vital matter, then it is not long before they are saying to themselves that other commands of God do not matter so much either, and that is the slippery slope to walking out on Christ. In my own experience I have seen a number of people who appeared to be zealous young Christians who today are spiritually nowhere through ignoring this vital command. This is how folk do come to be 'cut off' from God. This really is how people lose contact with God.

We know from the divorce statistics of today, with something like one in three marriages ending in divorce, that a marriage is a fragile thing. It is terribly important that the marriage partners have the deepest possible unity if that marriage is to last. If the partners are not agreed in this greatest matter of whether or not to live for Christ, it is a recipe for disaster. For both partners' sakes, for that of the Christian and of the non-Christian, it is better not to marry. No one wants a wrecked marriage.

You say, 'I'll marry him/her and he/she will be converted.' In God's great goodness that sometimes happens. But it is comparatively rare. The drift of Scripture is that it is far more likely the opposite will happen — you will backslide and even fall away. If it could happen to a godly man like King Solomon, it can happen to you (1 Kings 11:1—6).

Besides, think of the hypocrisy involved in marrying a non-Christian and then trying to convert him or her. Conversion is coming to submit to the Lord Jesus Christ as your Master and King. How can someone who is flying directly in the face of God's command not to marry outside God's family then turn round and say to his or her partner, 'You ought to submit to Christ.' You are telling the other person to do something which you are not doing. It is sheer hypocrisy.

Sometimes two non-Christians are married and then later one of them is converted. That situation is very different from an unmarried Christian deliberately marrying a non-Christian. The Lord understands that situation and he is very tender about it. You were not deliberately breaking the unity of God's people when you married; you were not a Christian yourself. You were not breaking God's command; it did not apply to you then. It was the Lord who in his eternal plan decided that he would not call you to Christ until after your marriage and therefore you can rely upon him to give you extra strength and grace to cope with the situation and love your partner. The apostle Peter has some wise words for just this situation: 'Wives, in the same way be submissive to your husbands so that, if any of them do not believe the word, they may be won over without talk by the behaviour of their wives, when they see the purity and reverence of your lives' (1 Peter 3:1,2).

Some practical advice for single people

1. Perhaps you are asking the question: 'Well, I'm clear now on whom I should not marry, but if I am to get married, what sort of person should I be looking for?'

The apostle Paul was single, but he knew if ever he was to get married it would have to be to a 'believing wife' (1 Corinthians 9:5). You must look for a Christian.

But having said that, there is something else to say, because anyone can *say* they are a Christian. You might find someone who claims to be a Christian, but who is only saying that, perhaps even deceiving him/herself about it, because he/she is so keen to marry you. So for your good and for the other person's you have got to look for someone who gives more evidence of being a Christian than just saying so. In other words, look for someone who is showing definite evidence in his/her life of being zealous for Christ and cultivating the fruit of the Spirit. Look for a Christian who shows a definite growth in grace, who is involved in some way in evangelism, who has a prayer life and an obvious devotion to the Lord. Look for a Christian with whom you can talk about the things of God, with whom you can pray, someone you can respect for his/her faith. This matter of marriage is one of the biggest decisions in life. In many ways it will shape your future. Do not let anything sway you, especially wishful thinking or pity. Do not 'look through the eyes of love'; look through the eyes of Scripture. There will be plenty of years later for the eyes of love.

Robert Flockhart was a remarkable man who, after years as a soldier in India, had a great ministry of street preaching in the first half of the nineteenth century in and around Edinburgh. This is what he records of how he got married. 'About this time the words that God spoke after he made man, came into my mind — "It is not good for the man to be alone" — I was a single man and was about thirty-five years of age. I saw in the book of Proverbs, that "a prudent wife is from the Lord". I made prayer and supplication unto the Lord, that, if it was his will, he would direct me to one such as I have mentioned. I was to use the means and the person whom the Lord had appointed for me was to consent; and if I asked any that he had not appointed, she was to say no. There were no less than three that I spoke to, and they all refused, but the fourth consented. After I was married, she told me that she herself had prayed that, if it was the Lord's will that she should change her life, he would give her a praying husband or none at all. After we were a little while married, she burst into tears of joy, and said she had got her request; she had prayed for a praying husband, and she had got one sent her all the way from the East Indies. I had thus the pleasure of a praying wife, and we both gave thanks to the Lord for answering prayers. I thought that, being believers, if we acknowledged God in all our ways, he would direct our steps."[11]

These may be very quaint words, but they are beautiful.

Do you see Robert Flockhart's spiritual priorities. What is more important to you, that the person you marry should have good looks or be someone who walks with God? We should have nothing against good looks, but put them in perspective. The book of Proverbs says, 'Charm is deceptive, and beauty is fleeting; but a woman who fears the Lord is to be praised' (Proverbs 31:30).

2. Christ calls his followers to take up the cross and follow him. Suppose that it will turn out that there will be no Christian for you to marry, what are you going to do? This is hopefully a hypothetical situation, but it is worth facing. Are you prepared to stay single if that is the cost of being faithful to the Lord Jesus? Some people are endowed with a gift for singleness and the thought does not worry them in the least. That is good; such folk can often be enormously useful to the church of Christ with no family ties to worry them (1 Corinthians 7:25—35). But not many of us are made that way. We are like Adam. It is not good for us to be alone, and singleness for such people can be a very real cross to bear. Are we prepared to be obedient, even if it means pain?

Old spinsters in churches have often been the butt of many a sarcastic comment and joke. But many of those women of a passing era were young during the First World War. Many a Christian girl lost her Christian sweetheart in the trenches of Flanders and after the war there were no Christian men for them to marry. And there they were, years after, the subject of ridicule by the world. But, rather than compromise their commitment to Christ and marry a non-Christian, they remained faithful to their Lord. We will find that many of those spinsters are recognized by the Lord in heaven as spiritual heroines. The Lord is mindful of such loving sacrifice for him; he is mindful of the tears and the heartache and he will not let such devotion go unrewarded. Are you prepared to carry the cross for Christ? You will probably never have to face the kind of situation that those women faced. Even if there were another war the methods of war are very different now from those of seventy years ago. But have you resolved to be faithful to Christ, come what may?

3. The gift of singleness (1 Corinthians 7:7) is the ability to live a single life while remaining emotionally stable and sexually pure. If you are a Christian of marriageable age and you know in yourself that you do not have the gift of singleness then it is not wrong to think about taking some positive steps towards marrying a Christian.

Now this is not the place for a full development of this subject but one practical comment is worth making. We have thought about the kind of person you should be looking for if you want to get married. But it is also more than worthwhile to turn the question around and ask yourself, 'Am I the sort of person that a good Christian would want to marry?'

There are good Christian girls, like the lady who married Robert Flockhart, who are looking for a praying husband. Are you a man of prayer? Are you a person who is found regularly in the secret place with God? Perhaps one of the most practical steps for some towards getting married is overhauling their daily times of Bible reading and prayer. Perhaps you ask, 'Why doesn't God lead me to the person I can marry?' and perhaps the answer is that your spiritual life is in such a desperate state that the Lord feels unable at present to entrust one of his children yet to a life shared with you.

Young man, a Christian young woman is looking for someone to marry, who is not perfect, but who bears some approximation to the kind of husband a Christian is called to be, as Paul sets out in Ephesians: 'Husbands, love your wives, just as Christ loved the church and gave himself up for her to make her holy, cleansing her by the washing with water through the word, and to present her to himself as a radiant church, without stain or wrinkle or any other blemish, but holy and blameless' (Ephesians 5:25–27). Christ loved the church before she was perfect, he bears with her faults and he gave himself on the cross to do her good. He was prepared to sacrifice his life, his personal needs, in order to bless her. Ask God to help you grow up in Christ that you might begin to be such a man who is fit to be a prophet, priest and king to a Christian family.

Young lady, a zealous Christian young man is looking for someone to marry who bears something of the character of feminine godliness as set out, for example, in 1 Peter 3: 'Your beauty should not come from outward adornment, such as braided hair and the wearing of gold jewellery and fine clothes. Instead, it should be that of your inner self, the unfading beauty of a gentle and quiet spirit, which is of great worth in God's sight. For this is the way the holy women of the past who put their hope in God used to make themselves beautiful' (1 Peter 3:3—5). A good Christian man does not drool over the ungodly pin-ups of the glossy magazines. But many a Christian young fellow drools over the description presented by Peter in those verses and thinks to himself, 'Oh, to meet a girl like that! Oh, not just to have a description of her, but to meet a walking, talking, living example of those verses! That would be the girl for me!'

This matter of finding a marriage partner can be a very difficult time for some. But we are to submit to the Word of God and wait upon the loving purposes of our Father. 'No good thing does he withhold from those whose walk is blameless. O Lord Almighty, blessed is the man who trusts in you' (Psalm 84:11).

7.
Guard your spirit

Please read Malachi 2:13—16

We can imagine a man coming to the prophet Malachi, spiritually concerned and asking for a private interview, as people do with their pastors and elders. 'Malachi, my spiritual life seems to be totally dry. I feel barren and lifeless. I have a Christian wife and family, I'm regular at church, I do my best to persevere with Bible reading, but I'm getting nothing out of it. I've cried to God again and again in prayer, but it is as if he's not there. He doesn't seem to answer me. My faith has lost its reality. Why, Malachi? What's gone wrong?' And Malachi's reply is 'How are things between you and your wife?' Perhaps the man gets a little annoyed. 'I've come here to bare my soul and seek spiritual counsel about my prayer life and you are asking me about my marriage? What sort of counsellor are you, Malachi? What's my marriage got to do with my private prayer life?' But Malachi says, 'I'm dead serious. How are things in your marriage?'

We are studying Malachi and we have been brought to consider the question of how people seem to lose contact with God. There was much hollow religion and empty formalism in the worship of God in Malachi's time. How does that happen? How do people let slip a vital relationship with the living God?

Already Malachi has laid down one major principle which governs the verses we are now considering. Frequently a vital relationship with God fades into barrenness and stagnation when a person deals faithlessly with others of God's people. If we do not do all we can to preserve and stimulate the unity and love of God's true people, then we

73

are heading for trouble. This is one of the reasons why in the New Testament the apostle Paul gives frequent and fervent pleas for unity and love among born-again Christians. 'If you have any encouragement from being united with Christ, if any comfort from his love, if any fellowship with the Spirit, if any tenderness and compassion, then make my joy complete by being like-minded, having the same love, *being one in spirit and purpose*' (Philippians 2:1,2 see also 1 Corinthians 1:10; 12:25; 2 Corinthians 13:11; Ephesians 4:1–6; Philippians 4:2; Colossians 3:15 etc.) Oneness of mind and heart among true Christians has a very high priority. It is not the only priority in the Christian life. But it certainly is a priority. People run straight into trouble with God through sinful actions and attitudes towards other Christians.

Christian marriage

'Now', Malachi is saying to our imaginary person he is counselling, 'don't you realize that this same principle applies within your Christian marriage? Don't you realize that this general rule applies as much to your attitudes towards your husband or your wife as it does towards any other person? That is why, in answer to your question about spiritual barrenness, I'm asking you about the state of your marriage.' When Jesus taught us to pray, 'Forgive us our sins as we also forgive everyone who sins against us,' that includes our wives. When Paul says, 'Do not grieve the Holy Spirit . . . get rid of all bitterness, rage and anger . . .' that applies to what you think and say about your husband as well as to everyone else in the church.

So it is, again by way of answer to the question as to why the Lord was not answering their prayers that Malachi writes, **'You ask, "Why?" It is because the Lord is acting as the witness between you and the wife of your youth, because you have broken faith with her, though she is your partner, the wife of your marriage covenant'** (2:14).

Now in the light of this matter of faithlessness in marriage

God says, 'So guard yourself in your spirit, and do not break faith with the wife of your youth' (2:15). Then, to underline that, he says again in the next verse, 'So guard yourself in your spirit, and do not break faith' (2:16). Thankfully, it is still comparatively rare for people from Bible-believing, gospel-preaching churches to fall into the sin of physically committing adultery. But the matter of the thought life, the life of the inner spirit, is much more of a problem. '**Guard yourself in your spirit.**'

From this repeated injunction we learn one very clear lesson. It is this: *a frequent cause of spiritual barrenness in a person is a thought life which violates his or her marriage*. So it is that God calls upon us to guard our spirits.

Let me remind you that the Lord has access to our thoughts. They are all read by him. Our thoughts might be hidden from men, and we are glad that they are, but they are not hidden at all from God. Consider some of the fundamental Bible statements about this: 'O Lord, you have searched me and you know me. You know when I sit and when I rise; you perceive my thoughts from afar . . . Before a word is on my tongue you know it completely, O Lord' (Psalm 139:1–4). 'The word of God is living and active. Sharper than any double-edged sword . . . it judges the thoughts and attitudes of the heart. Nothing in all creation is hidden from God's sight. Everything is uncovered and laid bare before the eyes of him to whom we must give account' (Hebrews 4:12,13).

These statements are plain. 'But', perhaps we ask, 'can it really be that God is all that concerned about what goes on in our heads? After all, nobody is immediately hurt by what we think.' The answer is again that God takes the sins of our thought life very seriously indeed. Remember Jesus' words: 'You have heard that it was said, "Do not commit adultery." But I tell you that anyone who looks at a woman lustfully has already committed adultery with her in his heart. If your right eye causes you to sin, gouge it out and throw it away. It is better for you to lose one part of your body than for your whole body to be thrown into hell' (Matthew 5:27–29). Again, if we enquire into

the reasons the Bible gives for God sending the terrible judgement of the flood in Noah's time to destroy nearly all mankind, we find the following: 'The Lord saw how great men's
wickedness on the earth had become, and that every incli-
nation of the thoughts of his heart was only evil all the
time . . . So the Lord said, "I will wipe mankind . . . off
from the face of the earth"' (Genesis 6:5–7). God is
desperately concerned and extremely angered by a sinful
thought life. It should not surprise us to find Malachi warning us that a thought life which violates our marriage can
cause God to withdraw his blessing from us.

In these verses of Malachi's prophecy it does not specify
any particular kind of extra-marital thought or attitude
which violates God's commands concerning marriage. We
must take it that *any* such thought is an offence to God.

Perhaps you are a recently married young man. As a
new employee at your place of work there comes a very
attractive girl and you let your mind drift back over the
possibilities that would have been open to you were you
not married. It is an offence to God.

Perhaps two married couples have begun to enjoy one
another's company and are regularly spending an evening
together. There is nothing wrong with that. That is
absolutely fine. But soon looking forward to those evenings
becomes something more than social. The physical
attraction of the other man's wife, the charm of the other
woman's husband begins to figure in an adulterous way in
the thought life of this partner and that partner. It is wrong.

But it is not just adulterous thinking that can be involved
here. Many marriages have a problem of bitterness. Many a
woman marries with high hopes for the future. But perhaps
your husband has not made such a success of his career
as was initially expected. That dream house in that idyllic
setting has not materialized and there is little hope that
it ever will. So now there is blame and bitterness. Perhaps
others have swallowed the half-truths of women's liberation,
and there is a wife who deep down is breaking her marriage
vows, saying to herself that she could have had a much better
life without him, she could have had her own career, without

the hassle of pregnancy and nappies and children. Even Christians can flirt with these thoughts and it is an avenue of thought which breaks the marriage covenant and brings about a withdrawing of God's fulness from our lives.

Again there is the other side of the coin. Perhaps there is a man who feels something of a failure in his marriage and career. Perhaps he feels that really he bit off more than he could chew in attempting this kind of career, and now he yearns for the past. If only life's choices were set before him again — and he is the kind of man who has a study or a woodshed where he disappears away from the family for hours on end. He is a man given to depression and he loves to get away and let his mind run riot in the fantasy world of what might have been without this marriage. Outwardly he is the most respectable and regular church attender you could wish to meet, but inwardly something is dreadfully wrong. He never misses a mid-week prayer meeting. But the real reason for this is not so spiritual. It is to get away from the family and be on his own again. All this is a thought life which deals faithlessly with that Christian marriage partner. The Lord looks upon all these things and many similar thoughts and is grieved and displeased. A frequent cause of spiritual barrenness is a thought life which violates your marriage.

There is a great temptation in our society, where divorce and adultery have horrifyingly become just an accepted part of the background to life, that we relax the standards of purity which the Word of God indicates to us. 'Oh, come on! Everybody gets fed up with their wife or husband! Everybody plays around with a few fantasies and extra-marital thoughts! Don't be such a hypocritical Puritan!' We would be hypocrites if we made out that these things never entered our heads or never presented any temptation to us. But the point is, are we fighting them, are we earnestly striving to put them to death, or are we tolerating and nurturing them?

In verses 14 to 16 Malachi helps us to have more insight into why we, unlike others in the world, should regard these sinful thoughts very seriously. The verses indicate three activities of God with respect to our marriages.

The Lord witnesses (2:14)
'The Lord is acting as the witness between you and the wife of your youth, because you have broken faith with her.'

Some of the Jews needed to face up to the way they were thinking and acting towards their wives. Paraphrasing again for a moment, God was saying to them, 'Your wife is the wife of your youth. She gave herself to you in the bloom of youth. She has given you the best years of her life, but now that the years have rolled by and there are grey hairs and a few wrinkles you think that you can cast her off like some old shoe, and perhaps take one of those Egyptian women from down the way! You cast her off in your thoughts. She has left the love of her parents' home for you. She has been your companion, your helper, your friend. She has lifted you up when you felt depressed. She has cared for you and now you want to divorce her in your thoughts!'

But what such a person forgets, be he a Jewish contemporary of Malachi, or a product of sophisticated twentieth-century society, is that marriage is not man's invention; it is God's institution (Genesis 2:18,24). What people forget is that when they married, they made a covenant, they gave a promise, not just before the registrar or the vicar, but before the living God. God witnessed that contract between man and wife and will take action against any of his people who begin to stray from their promise. If you are married, do you remember whose are the signatures upon your marriage certificate? Malachi is reminding us that in a very real way the signature of God is upon that certificate.

Do you remember what promises you made on that marvellous occasion? You did not promise simply to live in the same house as your partner for the rest of your lives. You promised 'to love and to cherish'. The dictionary definition of 'cherish' is 'to nurse', 'to hold dear', 'to protect and treat with fondness or kindness', 'to keep in one's mind and heart'. You promised to give your partner an exclusive loving place in your thoughts. You promised to be married not just in body, but in spirit. The Lord was a witness to that and now with a thought life which violates what you expressly promised, the Lord will take action. If you play around with thoughts of separation from your wife or husband, God will let you know what it is like for you to live separate from him. He withdraws his fellowship. What a fitting act of discipline! Of course, for is not your marriage a picture of the relationship between Christ and the church, between your soul and your God?

The Lord seeks (2:15)

'Has not the Lord made them one? In flesh and in spirit they are his. And why one? Because he was seeking godly offspring. So guard yourself in your spirit and do not break faith with the wife of your youth.'

The original language of the Old Testament is difficult to understand here. It could mean what the Authorized Version says, 'Yet had he the residue of the Spirit.' If this is the original meaning perhaps we are to understand that by the power of the Spirit through which God created mankind, God could have made more than one partner for the man (or vice versa). But he chose not to, in his wisdom, and therefore the one-to-one pattern of marriage is normative.

The New International Version translates it as, 'In flesh and in spirit they are his,' reminding us, as we have emphasized already, that God is not simply interested in the outward appearance of a marriage, but in the inner love, companionship and devotion expressed.

But the verse indicates that God is seeking something from these Jewish marriages. Just so, he is seeking something from all godly marriages. He is seeking godly offspring. He is looking for our children to become disciples. Of course, there is no guarantee that children of Christian parents will automatically embrace the faith of their parents (John 3: 5–8; Luke 12:51–53; 1 Timothy 3:4,12). But we must realize that an unhappy Christian marriage, where the thought life (and therefore probably the words and actions) of the partners is far from perfect harmony, will be a profound obstacle to our children becoming Christians.

Where does the child get his first impressions of what the Father in heaven is like? Surely his idea of fatherhood must be coloured by what he sees of his own father. Our marriages are meant to present to our children a picture of the relationship between Christ and the church. What do they see? Touchiness? Sniping? One partner spending time alone as often as possible? One partner for whom the career means more than the marriage?

Our marriages are like a fig tree from which our Lord is expecting fruit. Our marriages are not just for us. They are for the Lord. Does he come to our marriages expecting to find refreshing fruit, but like that fig tree in the Gospels find none, though he had every reason to expect fruit? Why does he find no fruit? Sometimes it is *not* the Christian parents' fault that children rebel. We are all sinners. But sometimes a heavy responsibility for the child's rebellion against the things of God lies with the parents. Sometimes it is the parents' fault. They have brought the name of God into disrepute with the child through what the child has seen in the marriage. That is terribly serious and we should not be surprised that God withdraws.

Unhelpful actions and words within a marriage begin in the minds of the partners. So God is saying, 'Guard your spirit' in this matter.

The Lord hates (2:16)

' "I hate divorce," says the Lord God of Israel, "and I hate a man's covering himself with violence as well as with his garment," says the Lord Almighty.'

The basic attitude of God towards divorce is summed up in this verse: 'I hate divorce.' What does it mean? Does it mean that in God's view there is never any place for divorce at all and that Christians should campaign against all divorce legislation? If we look at the totality of biblical data, the answer seems to be no. Because of the sinfulness of people's hearts, and to curtail the kind of dreadful misery which sinful people can inflict upon one another when they are locked together in a hateful marriage, God did allow for divorce in the words he gave to Moses. God is gracious towards the innocent party in a divorce (Matthew 5:31,32), but basically God finds divorce obnoxious. 'I hate divorce.' In other words, God wishes that there never had to be such a thing as divorce. All divorce is occasioned by sin somewhere along the line. At best it is the lesser of two evils and God wishes there was no evil.

God does not view divorce as our present society does. It is not a trivial matter to him. One of the reasons for that is that all divorces are both a symptom and a symbol of the great divorce between God and man and of adulterous fallen mankind going after other gods (James 4:4). Again God hates it because, according to Jesus, divorce is a direct undoing of the work of God: 'For this reason a man will leave his father and mother and be united to his wife, and the two will become one flesh. So they are no longer two, but one. Therefore what God has joined together, let not man separate' (Matthew 19:5,6). God is grieved by the whole thing and all divorce, Malachi reminds us, begins in the heart and mind. 'So guard yourself in your spirit.'

The seriousness with which God views it is brought out by Malachi as in verse 16 he equates divorce with violence. In God's eyes, these extra-marital thoughts are just as bad as preparing to attack someone. Those 'innocent' little thoughts which 'playfully' stray over the boundary lines of marriage are equivalent in God's sight to the thoughts of a villain who is planning grievous bodily harm on somebody.

Let us be blunt. Church-going, respectable people can be a very strange breed. They are so respectable that even their fantasies must have an air of respectability. Aren't there some Christians who in their extra-marital fantasies, wishing to avoid the stigma of adultery, have considered the possibility of their partner dying, and in that fantasy have stood by the very graveside of that partner with the thought of now being free to move on their way, free to go to that other woman, or that other man? How do you think such thoughts appear in the sight of a holy God? Do not be surprised that he equates such thoughts with the worst violence! Do not be surprised that your spiritual life is at a low ebb if you are happy to entertain such thoughts! With such thoughts in your mind it is only of God's enormous grace that you have any spiritual life at all! It is time for repentance!

Can we see then that a frequent cause of losing vital contact with the living God is a thought life which violates our marriages? So God comes to us through the prophet Malachi and earnestly says to us, 'Guard yourself in your spirit and do not break faith.'

The practice of guarding our spirits

If we acknowledge the need for holy minds, then immediately we are faced with a question. The Lord says that we should guard our spirits. But how are we to go about this? Our minds are so easily invaded. How are we to seek to maintain the purity and exclusivity of our marriages even in our thought life?

Here are four suggestions which you may find helpful.

1. *Recognize the problem of these thoughts*
You must face up to this problem personally and look it in the eye. You may not like to admit to yourself that you have this problem. If you do not suffer from this particular sin — excellent! But if you do, you must be honest with yourself and face it squarely. You will never master it unless you regard it as an enemy. It is not neutral or acceptable; it is an enemy of the well-being of your spiritual life. Start staring it in the eye. Al Martin likens this to the days of the old Wild West, when two gunfighters would face each other down the main street. They watched each other like hawks. The man who took his eyes off his enemy to raise his hat and say, 'How do you do?' to passers by was dead.[12] We will know the deadness and barrenness of spiritual life if we treat sin lightly in any way.

2. *Recognize the kind of family situations which promote disunity between you and your partner and do something about them*
Often it can be quite small irritations between marriage partners which ignite and catalyse adulterous or bitter thoughts. If there is some regular source of irritation between

partners then this needs to be sorted out in some way and avoided if possible.

Martin Luther and his wife struggled with quite a modern kind of problem within their marriage. 'Part of the difficulty was that the rhythm of work and rest did not coincide for Luther and his wife. After a day with children, animals, and servants, she wanted to talk with an equal; and he, after preaching four times, lecturing and conversing with students at meals, wanted to drop into a chair and sink into a book. Then Katie would start in, "Herr Doktor, is the prime minister of Prussia the Duke's brother?"

"All my life is patience," said Luther. "I have to have patience with the pope, the heretics, my family, and Katie." '[13]

Does this kind of thing sound a little familiar for the tired commuting office worker and the wife who is wedded to the world of children? We need to work at such seemingly small but regular causes of friction. Partners need to understand and help one another. Luther needs his mental relaxation and Katie needs her mental stimulation. They need to work the thing out so that the devil is not given a foothold.

3. *Take any appropriate action to eradicate the sin*
The words of Jesus, which we have already seen and which relate to just this area, are radical. 'If your right eye causes you to sin, gouge it out and throw it away. It is better for you to lose one part of your body than for your whole body to be thrown into hell' (Matthew 5:29). We are to treat adulterous thoughts as a matter of spiritual life or death. We are to go to any lengths to deal with them.

Are there certain places or certain people which stimulate sinful thoughts in you? Then avoid them. Is there some private memento you keep from perhaps your schooldays which reminds you of some long lost sweetheart and around which extra-marital fantasies revolve? Then it is time for it to be consigned to the dustbin. Are you plagued with thoughts from the past, perhaps of some immoral relationship you had with someone before you became a Christian?

Then it is time to plead with God that he would deaden those memories and make them as repugnant to you as they are to him.

It is of great practical help to pray and meditate over the warnings of Scripture in this area. Think of the terrible consequences of a broken marriage and adultery, which Satan hides from you as you are tempted to contemplate it. Look at dear friends, who perhaps live in your neighbourhood and who now live with the torment of a broken marriage. Look at those who have gone through divorce and come out the other side hard and callous. Look at the heartbroken children who are with dad one weekend and mum the next. Make yourself think about these things and it will have a good effect. Consider the wise words of Scripture. 'It will save you also from the adulteress, from the wayward wife with her seductive words, who has left the partner of her youth and ignored the covenant she made before God. For her house leads down to death and her path to the spirits of the dead. None who go to her return or attain the path of life' (Proverbs 2:16—19). 'Can a man scoop fire into his lap without his clothes being burned? Can a man walk on hot coals without his feet being scorched? So is he who sleeps with another man's wife; no one who touches her will go unpunished . . . But a man who commits adultery lacks judgement; whoever does so destroys himself. Blows and disgrace are his lot, and his shame will never be wiped away; for jealousy arouses a husband's fury, and he will show no mercy when he takes revenge' (Proverbs 6:27—34). (See also Proverbs 5:1—23; 7:1—27; 9:13—18; 22:14; 23:26—28; 30:18—20; Galatians 5:19—21; 1 Thessalonians 4:3—8).

4. *Work at improving the loving relationship within your marriage*
In Malachi 2:14 a Hebrew word is used which means a close friend with whom interests good and bad are shared. It is used here of a wife. The very essence of marriage is friendship and companionship. We should not allow the friendship which blossomed in our youthful marriage to become jaded by the passage of time and the events of life.

The old Puritan Thomas Watson wrote, 'A man is not kept chaste by having a wife, but by *loving* his wife.' What a refreshing delight it is when occasionally we come across folk who have been married for twenty or thirty years who are still head over heels in love with each other! That is how every Christian marriage should be. Contrary to the opinions of the glossy magazines, such marriages are not a matter of luck. They do not just happen. They are made by perseverance and patience and thought and love. Practical steps may need to be taken — perhaps a baby-sitter or two so that you can spend time out just being together. It is not wrong to go to God in prayer and ask him for grace to help you keep those marriage vows and help you love your husband or love your wife.

Once or twice over the last couple of years I have come across reports of Satanists specifically praying against Christian marriages. They recognize that good Christian marriages are the strength of the church. How we need to work and pray! God says, 'Guard yourself in your spirit, and do not break faith with the wife of your youth.'

8.
The refiner's fire

Please read Malachi 2:17—3:5

The picture of the ancient refiner of silver going about his task is both a very beautiful picture and a very sobering one for the Christian.

You will remember the old-fashioned refining process. The metal was brought to a high temperature so that it melted. Then the impurities in the metal, which have a lower density than the metal itself, would float to the top of the molten liquid and could be blown with bellows from the surface. This process was carefully repeated until there was purity.

The beauty of the picture is in the fact that when the refiner of silver had done his work thoroughly then towards the end of the process the thin covering of oxide disappeared and the pure bright surface of the silver flashed out. At that point, when all the dross had gone, the refiner could see his own reflection on the surface of the purified silver. What a marvellous thing it is that God is working in the lives of all Christians, seeking to refine them from sin and transforming us into his own likeness! (Colossians 3:10 etc.) Our hearts leap a little to think of this. What a privilege that this process should be going on in us as God seeks to make us to be closer and closer approximations to the likeness of our Lord Jesus Christ!

The seriousness and sobriety of this same picture of purification, however, is that this refining process takes place by *fire*. It is no comfortable process. It is a process of destruction, involving scorching heat and devouring flames. It is through many troubles that Christian character and faith are developed (Romans 5:4,5). It is through facing trials of all kinds that our sinful impatience is dealt with and Christ-like patience blossoms (James 1:2—4). It is through taking up the cross that we become more like Christ. We are refined by fire.

In this section of the book of Malachi the prophet, like others before him, speaks about God refining and purifying his people like an ancient refiner of precious metals (cf Isaiah 1:25; 48:10; Jeremiah 6:29,30; Ezekiel 22:17—22). 'He will sit as a refiner and purifier of silver; he will purify the Levites and refine them like gold and silver' (3:3). He purifies Christians as *individuals* and he also purifies the *church*. There are times when the professing people of God have gone so far astray, and among them there are many folk who are not God's people at all. In such a situation God moves to sort things out. He acts to bring about a separation of the precious from the dross. It is chiefly with this corporate refining process that this passage is concerned.

The historical perspective

In Malachi we stand at the very end of the Old Testament. Malachi is the last in a long line of men who have spoken God's inspired words to the nation. Following Malachi there will be a long silence of some 400 years and when that silence is again broken it will be by the voice of John the Baptist announcing the coming of Christ, the setting aside of the old ways and the innovation of the new covenant. We stand on the very brink of this grand revolution in the things of God. One far greater than Abraham or Moses was about to appear. The animal sacrifices would be swept away and atonement totally consummated once and for all in the cross of Christ. God's people would no longer be one small nation but a world-wide church from every nation. The Holy Spirit would be poured out and free salvation preached to all in the name of the risen Lord Jesus Christ.

This passage in Malachi presents us with a biblical perspective on the end of Old Testament Jewish religion and the

ministry of the Lord Jesus Christ particularly as it pertained
to the Jews.

The situation in Judah (2:17)

The beginning of verse 17 shows us that we are at a major
crossroads in the history of the Jews. We have reached a
watershed. We are confronted with something totally out
of the ordinary and extremely serious. We read, 'You have
wearied the Lord.'

There is no divine attribute more wonderful than the
patience of God. His patience with various wayward
characters, like Jacob and Lot, throughout the Old Testament, is extraordinary. Some people wonder why God
allows the world to go on with all its sin. Why hasn't he
brought it to an end sooner? The apostle Peter explains that
it is because of his enormous patience. He is slow to anger.
He defers the Day of Judgement and the end of the world,
giving sinners every opportunity to repent (2 Peter 3:9).
What patience!

But here in Malachi the prophet explains that we have
come to a point where God considers the situation among
the Jews irretrievable. We are confronted with a situation
in which the prophet has been instructed to tell the nation
that God has had enough. God's patience had run out, as
it were. From this we must infer the extreme nature of
the situation. We indeed stand at the *end* of the Old Testament as we read Malachi.

What is the situation? So far we have seen that Malachi
was prophesying at a time when the nation of Israel was
spiritually at a very low ebb. The people's worship was an
empty charade. The priests, the spiritual leaders, were bored
time-servers who could not be bothered. The nation was
flouting God's commands generally about honesty, but
especially concerning what he had said about marriage.
But now we see something far worse was present — stubborn,
God-accusing self-righteousness.

Two great factors played upon the minds of Malachi's
contemporaries. The *first* was that, although the temple
had been rebuilt, there had been no supernatural manifestation

of God coming to dwell in the new temple as there had been at the consecration of the first temple in the days of Solomon (1 Kings 8:10,11). Although prophets like Haggai had promised, as they foresaw the coming of Jesus and his ministry within their new temple, that the glory of this second temple would eventually be greater than that of the first, Malachi's contemporaries had no faith to believe it (Haggai 2:9). They longed for the cloud of God's glory to come in the old way and inwardly they resented God not doing that. It hurt their pride that God had not given them what he had given to others, and they were more interested in their pride than in God's will and God's plans for the future.

The *second* matter which irritated the Jews of Malachi's day was their poverty in comparison with the great days of their kingdom in the past. They self-righteously felt that they had done enough to warrant God's blessing. They looked at the apparent prosperity of wicked nations and wicked individuals around them, then they looked at their own difficulties, and they were envious and they were bitter against God. Although they were not saying it out loud, yet in their hearts they were thinking, 'All who do evil are good in the eyes of the Lord,' and again, 'Where is the God of justice?' (2:17.)

Self-righteously they were saying to themselves, 'How dare God withhold his blessing from us? It is those wicked people over there he ought to be judging, not us! Oh, how we wish God would come in justice!' They were so self-righteous that they were ready to accuse God of being unjust, rather than ever contemplating the possibility that they might be in the wrong. Rather than having faith to see that a loving God was seeking to bring them to repentance through their troubles, they were vicious against God. 'How dare God keep us poor and leave us under the domination of Persia?'

What made things worse was the fact that God's gracious intentions towards the nation through trouble were plainly discernible from the past. All they had to do in order to see what God was doing was to read their history books. Again and again they could read of how God had sent them trouble in the form of bad harvests, wars, bad kings, droughts and all manner of things, whenever he was graciously calling them back from sin to fidelity to his covenant. Indeed, less than 100 years before these people could look back and see God's dealings with them in just this way through the exile in Babylon. The nation had been flouting his covenant and he had chastised them for their good, but then, just as he had promised, he had brought them back. Indeed, at the very founding of the covenant between Israel and God in the days of Moses, God had explained that he would lovingly deal with them in this way to seek to keep them true to their promises as a nation. But, in spite of all this, in spite of all that God had explained, in spite of all the examples from their own history, they refused to have faith in God in their comparatively light difficulties. Instead they rather interpreted their situation in such a way as to support unspoken atheism or to accuse God.

Through all the history of God's dealings with the nation they had learned precisely nothing. They were just the same as those first stiff-necked grumblers who complained against God in the days of Moses in the wilderness. As regards educating the nation, it was as if God now felt he had completely wasted his time. The heart of the nation was as hard and as callous as ever, and now God was saying, 'Enough is enough; it is time for drastic action.' That drastic action was ultimately to include the passing of the Old Testament and the bringing in of the New.

God's response (3:1–5)

'Why doesn't God come and judge these oppressive Persians who dominate our land? Why doesn't God come and fill our temple with the cloud of his manifest glory? Why doesn't God come and prove us right?'

Malachi's reply to these self-righteous questions was something very different from what the Jews were expecting. He says that the Lord will come suddenly to his temple. **'See, I will send my messenger, who will prepare the way before me. Then suddenly the Lord you are seeking will** come to his temple; the messenger of the covenant, whom you desire, will come' (2:1). But when he does come, he will come first of all not to judge others, but *to judge his people*. He will come to purify and restore the true worship of God. 'But who can endure the day of his coming? Who can stand when he appears? For he will be like a refiner's fire or a launderer's soap. He will sit as a refiner and purifier of silver; he will purify the Levites and refine them like gold and silver. Then the Lord will have men who will bring offerings in righteousness, and the offerings of Judah and Jerusalem will be acceptable to the Lord, as in days gone by, as in former years' (3:2—4). When he does come he will come to judge you and people like you! Also at the same time, when God comes, he will put right the kind of evils the Jews have been complaining of in such a self-righteous way. God may not work to our time schedule, but in his own time he will balance the scales of justice. Malachi affirms the ultimate justice of God: ' "So I will come near to you for judgement. I will be quick to testify against sorcerers, adulterers and perjurers, against those who defraud labourers of their wages, who oppress the widows and the fatherless, and deprive aliens of justice, but do not fear me," says the Lord Almighty' (3:5). Many of the sins listed here were being perpetrated in Israel. One of the reasons for which God had chosen Israel and made a covenant with them was that they might be a holy nation and so an example and witness to the Gentile nations around them. But the sins listed in verse 5 show that, rather than being different and so challenging the Gentiles to seek God, Israel had fallen into the same sins as other nations. They were indistinguishable from the world. Also these social and industrial sins were other ways in which the people within Israel were sinning against each other and so profaning the covenant (cf. 2:10). These words sounded a stern warning in the ears of the people. God was going to come, but not in the way they, in their hard-hearted self-righteousness, were expecting.

God's judgement upon Judah began right away in the days of Malachi, whose name means 'my messenger' (3:1), with the fact that the Lord stopped speaking to his people. He sent no more prophets for 400 years. But ultimately, according to the New Testament, we are to understand God's response to Judah in terms of the ministry and mission of our Lord Jesus Christ. God waited until the hypocritical self-righteousness apparent in Malachi's time had come to its full bitter fruit in the Pharisaical Judaism of the first century A.D.

In one sense Malachi himself is 'my messenger' who prepares the way for the coming of Jesus. He is the last prophet of the Old Testament and the next page in our Bibles begins the Gospel of Matthew and the New Testament. No other vocational prophet opened his mouth after Malachi until the Lord Jesus Christ had been born into the world at Bethlehem.

But, of course, the New Testament makes it plain that these words concerning the messenger have a double reference. Our Lord, speaking of John the Baptist, takes up the words of Malachi 3:1 and says, 'This is the one about whom it is written: "I will send my messenger ahead of you, who will prepare your way before you"' (Matthew 11:10). John the Baptist was like a herald going before the royal procession to indicate the route that the king would take and to make preparations for his coming. The king was Jesus, God in the flesh. But Jesus himself was also a messenger. As well as being God's Son, he was the Prophet, 'the messenger of the covenant (3:1), who announced the new covenant.

Malachi tells us that one of the primary purposes of Jesus' ministry would be to purify the worship of God. This, as we now know, would include God's revolutionary transformation of Old Testament religion into Christianity. But Malachi expresses this great change in worship in words which the Jews of his day would more easily grasp, in terms of the purification of the priesthood and the bringing of righteous offerings (3:3,4). Christ is the great, pure Priest, who offered the righteous sacrifice to God which totally dealt with our sins. Christians are the new royal priesthood, who offer the acceptable sacrifices of praise (1 Peter 2:9).

Malachi's language would, of course, also speak convictingly to the situation of the sloppy, unsacrificial Old Testament worship of his own time (cf 1:6—14).

Jesus came to purify the people and the worship of God. Look how the messenger John the Baptist describes our Lord's ministry among the Jews: 'The axe is already at the root of the trees, and every tree that does not produce good fruit will be cut down and thrown into the fire. I baptize you with water for repentance. But after me will come one who is more powerful than I, whose sandals I am not fit to carry. He will baptize you with the Holy Spirit and with fire. His winnowing fork is in his hand, and he will clear his threshing floor, gathering wheat into his barn and burning up the chaff with unquenchable fire' (Matthew 3:10—12). Whereas these words must not be restricted purely to the Jews, since Jesus did come to judge all men, yet they were originally spoken to those who were resting their hopes on being able to say that, in the physical sense, 'We have Abraham as our father' (Matthew 3:9).

Jesus brought a great purging, refining, purifying and renewing of the worship of God. He was like the launderer. He was like the refiner of silver and gold, coming to get rid of the dirt and the dross in a thorough process of cleansing (3:2,3).

This great ministry of our Lord Jesus Christ is easily discernible in the Gospels. His penetrating corrections of the Pharisaic deviations from the plain commands of God ring through the beginning of the Sermon on the Mount: 'You have heard it said . . . But I tell you . . .' His withering descriptions of the Pharisees praying on the street corners to be seen by other people, or praying to themselves, thanking God that they were better than other people, either brought people to repentance or hardened them in their bigotry. The precious silver and the dross were being sorted out. His parable which spoke of wicked tenant farmers, who were misusing the owner's inheritance, was really about the Pharisees using religion and the people of God for their own ends instead of looking after them. He pointed plainly to their sins, calling them hypocrites, blind guides and whitewashed tombs. The refining fire of our Lord's scorching teaching was at work among the Jews, bringing forth the pure gold of sincere folk whose hearts belonged to God, but consuming the hypocritical rubbish. It is interesting to realize that plenty of such fiery teaching was given just as Malachi pictures it, within the confines of the temple courts (cf Matthew 23:1–39; 24:1). The final words of Jesus, as he left the temple for the last time to go to the cross at the hands of the self-righteous religious authorities, were 'Look, your house is left to you desolate. For I tell you, you will not see me again until you say, "Blessed is he who comes in the name of the Lord"' (Matthew 23:38,39). Without turning to Christ, Judaism was left as a hollow lifeless shell, whereas within weeks the church was baptized mightily in the Holy Spirit at Pentecost and the whole worship of God transformed and renewed, and the gospel of God's incalculable love blossomed in the world. The Refiner had done his most excellent work!

The present perspective

Although we must say that the change between the Old and the New Testament is obviously a unique event, yet there is a lesson here of more general application to church history and to our own day. It is this: *God is prepared to go to drastic lengths to purify the lives of his Church and his worship.*

There are times when things sink to such a low state in the professing people of God that the Lord acts drastically, terribly, vehemently in order to refine his church.

What a tremendous turn around there was at the ministry of Jesus! Caiaphas and the Pharisees and Sadducees were all swept away in the fires of purification and only people like Nicodemus and the apostle Paul came through. In the plan of God, the great temple in Jerusalem was smashed to the ground by the Roman armies as they attacked Jerusalem in A.D. 70, while the church of believers in Jesus was multiplying in homes and meeting-places all over the Roman Empire. Here is purification.

We can look at the Reformation from the same perspective. Things had sunk so low. Here was the church with ungodly leaders living in sin and luxury and the Bible almost totally ignored. Here was the church to whom God had sent 'prophets' like John Wycliffe, John Hus, Savonarola and others, calling it back to holiness and walking by the Word of God. But here was a church which refused to be reformed. Here were popes and priests submerged in gross immorality and avarice, who stopped their ears and burned God's men at the stake. So with the coming of Luther and his ninety-five theses of 1517 God's time had come for drastic action — the rending of the church.

What is God looking for in particular in his process of refining? We need to answer that question for ourselves in our own time, that we might keep ourselves on the right lines. As he refines, as he considers *us*, what is uppermost in God's mind?

We can answer this question by comparing the things which the hypocritical people of Judah were concerned about with what God was concerned about.

The people of Judah were concerned about injustice (2:17) and the matters of adultery, black magic and industrial cheating reflected in 3:5. Now God is holy and he was not unconcerned about those things. They grieved him terribly. But what God was primarily concerned about was his temple (3:1), his covenant (3:1), the spiritual leadership (3:3) and the offerings of devotion to him (3:4). In other words, what God was concerned about first and foremost was the state of true love for him in the church.

Now in considering ancient Judah it may be artificial to distinguish too definitely between the nation and the church. But in the situation of the church in the twentieth century that separation is quite easy. If we ask the question therefore to our situation, 'Which is foremost in God's concern, the general morality of our nation, or the spirituality and love for him within the professing church?' Malachi points us very definitely to the latter. God's first concern is always the state of the church. That is why when God moves in refining he always begins at the church (1 Peter

4:17). What is God concerned to see first and foremost, as
he moves the wheels of history and brings his refining fires?
It is the church, alive with truth and in love with him!

We can lose sight of that. We are probably moral, respectable people. We would not be found fiddling the company
books or meeting the neighbour's wife. We are evangelical
Christians! But what about the true fervency of our devotion
to God? Of course, God is concerned that we be moral, but
he is concerned for much more than that.

We can lose sight of God's great concern. We should pray
for our country. But we can so easily fall into a self-righteous
prayer hardly distinguishable from the attitude of Malachi's
time: 'O Lord, look at the sins of our nation! We would
not be at all surprised if you were to come and judge our
land with its injustice and its terrible immorality. O Lord,
those people out there are ripe for judgement!' But although
God is concerned with the sin of the nation, he is more
concerned about the spirituality of the church. You say,
'We would not be at all surprised if God came to judge
Britain . . .', but perhaps Malachi would look at us and say,
'I would not be at all surprised if God does come and
judge . . . the church!' because we are content and com-
placent in evangelical respectability and morality, while the
most important thing in God's sight is heart devotion and
love to Christ. Perhaps we blame God if we have so little
warmth towards Jesus. Perhaps we blame God for not giving
us more of his Spirit, rather than breaking our hearts in
repentance at our own hardness and insensitivity.

What is God looking for in his refining process? He is
looking for much more than just outward purity. He is
looking for sincere worship and adoration. Does he find it
in you?

Suppose we now ask an even more pertinent question
about how God is refining his church today. What are the
instruments which God is using to preserve and to refine
the church today? He can use persecution as his refining
fire sometimes. But this is rare at the moment in the Western
world. At the local level he can send trouble to local congregations and even remove the candlestick completely because

a church has lost its first love (Revelation 2:5). But, generally speaking, there are three very potent forces at work among us today, which we need to consider briefly, as in God's providence he purifies us.

1. *Rapidity of change in society*
There is probably no era in history so marked by rapid progress as our own. The futuristic world seems constantly to be crashing into the present. Technology is changing the texture of our lives at an alarming rate. The question is constantly confronting the church: 'Are Christians going to strive to show forth the praises and glory of God in a faithful and relevant way in these continually changing times?' So often we can become tired of trying to keep up with the pace. Unemployment, the morality of medical interference with human embryos, computerized artificial intelligence – we are constantly being asked what is the Christian view of such things. How do we minister to a generation which has lost all respect and confidence in the Bible? How can we communicate the gospel to ordinary folk whose only reading is a tabloid newspaper? Facing the ever-changing challenges of our times, we can easily feel like hibernating into the past. But if we do, where is our concern that our God be glorified in the latter days of the twentieth century? Do we love God and long to see his name hallowed by all, or not? The refining fires of change can expose us as loving the old traditions of religion, rather than first of all loving God who, after all, controls history.

2. *The charismatic movement*
The charismatic movement is a highly controversial and highly diverse creature. Although it has touched all parts of the professing church, it still awaits a firm theological basis and many charismatic groups differ drastically from each other in their teachings. It would be unrealistic either to give a blanket condemnation or a blanket commendation of charismatic Christianity. There are terrible errors in some groups which must be avoided. However, surely God is challenging the church in one way, quite obviously through

this movement. One of the main thrusts, perhaps the main thrust, of the whole movement is that there must be vital, articulate, open, warm love for God. We are challenged not simply to attend church and to believe the right things, but to love God. By the way we respond to that plainly right emphasis, God is at work among the church as a whole, separating the dross from the gold. Are we happy to be content with anything less than joyful devotion and love to our Father in heaven? A refining process is going on.

3. *Doctrinal error and division*
Jesus speaks about false ideas and false Christs who, throughout the history of the church, would be used to test the church. He speaks of them spreading error in such a persuasive way that they would 'deceive the elect — if that were possible' (Mark 13:22). Today there are those who hold high ecclesiastical office who utterly deny the authority of Scripture and so practically cut out God's tongue. Today an increasing number of errors and deviations from the central truths of the Christian faith are being perpetrated, which do not square with the touchstone of the Bible. Through these terribly plausible corruptions of the truth, a sifting process, a refining process is going on. The elect will discern what is of God, but the foolish will be led away into error, to their eternal loss.

Similarly, Paul writes to the Corinthians, 'No doubt there have to be differences among you to show which of you have God's approval' (1 Corinthians 11:19). The Puritan Matthew Poole comments, 'God hath his wise end in suffering breaches and divisions, that such as are true and sincere Christians, opposing themselves to such violations of charity, might appear to be true and sincere, and to have the love of God dwelling, working, and prevailing in them.' To hold to the truth in a real spirit of love is a great test for us, through which God refines his true people. Love alone is not enough. Truth alone is not enough (James 2:19). But God's elect will hold them together. God is refining his church.

9.
Repentance, faith and floodgates

Please read Malachi 3:6—12

The writer Daniel Defoe seems to have been a converted man, and in his most famous novel, *Robinson Crusoe*, he makes a very perceptive comment about repentance. He writes, 'I have since often observed, how incongruous and irrational the common temper of mankind is . . . that they are not ashamed to sin, and yet are ashamed to repent; not ashamed of the action for which they ought justly to be esteemed fools, but are ashamed of the returning, which only can make them be esteemed wise men.'[14] The pride of ordinary men and women is often one of the greatest hindrances to their repenting and coming to Christ.

Pride can also be an enormous stumbling-block to the professed people of God repenting and returning to follow God as they ought. Perhaps you have heard the well-known 'Inflexible Man's Prayer': 'O Lord, grant that we may always be right, for thou knowest we will never change our minds.'[15] It would be humorous if it was not so serious. Very often we can adopt attitudes which are virtually indistinguishable from that 'prayer'. Repentance is rarely an easy thing, and is never an easy thing for proud people. In this section of the prophecy of Malachi we find the prophet seeking to motivate proud, cynical, self-righteous Judah to repent and return to the Lord.

We have seen that Malachi warned the nation that, because of their spiritual carelessness and pride, God would come in judgement, to carry out a fiery purification, a radical refining of his people. But in this section we learn that, even so, God would rather that did not have to happen. The Lord still longs to bless the nation, and if only they would repent of their ways, if only they would truly return to him, he would not come in judgement, but he would come, instead, in marvellous blessing. God is a God who delights in blessing rather than in judgement.

In this section three powerful arguments are brought to bear with the loving intention of motivating the proud, self-righteous nation to repentance.

A return (3:6,7)

In these verses we are told two facts about the heart of God which tenderly urge repentance upon these wayward Jews.

1. *God has not moved*
When you go along to the railway station and buy a return ticket, perhaps to London, the reason why you can buy a return ticket is because the place you start from is going to remain firmly where it is! Its position will not change. The idea of a return presupposes the constancy of the place you left behind. This is what God first of all underlines in this paragraph as he calls people to return to him. They need to return to him because it is not he who has changed. It is they who have changed and gone off into their own ways. He has remained constant. **'I the Lord do not change. So you, O descendants of Jacob, are not destroyed'** (3:6).

God is constant *in his purpose for the nation*. He remains fixed in it. Through Abraham's physical descendants the Messiah would come and through him the whole world would be blessed. That was God's fixed intention. Abraham's grandson Jacob was a devious, sly, cunning man. He had cheated his brother out of his birthright. He cheated his uncle Laban. He was a conniving man, ever plotting and planning to benefit himself and God had a long struggle with Jacob to cure him of his ways. In verse 6, God is saying that the people of Judah in Malachi's day were descendants of Jacob, not just physically but in their cheating and insincere attitudes. God is saying, 'If I were not a constant God, constant to my purpose and promise, I would have every reason to cast you off for ever. The very fact that you are spared, that you are not destroyed, proves my constancy.'

'Ever since the time of your forefathers you have turned away from my decrees and have not kept them' (3:7). God is constant *in his commands.* God is not a God who keeps changing what he requires of his people. His standards have always been the same. It is not as if one day he requires one thing and the next day another. It is not as if he changes his commands from one generation to another. His requirements that his people exercise faith and maintain an honest struggle to live holy lives have always been the same. It is the people who have changed. It is they who have turned away from God's commands and have not kept them.

' "Return to me, and I will return to you," says the Lord Almighty' (3:7). God is constant *in his desire to do them good.* God yearns for them to return that he may bless them with his presence again. This constancy of desiring their good is underlined by the fact that the Lord had previously said exactly the same words as are contained in this verse about fifty years before by his prophet Zechariah (Zechariah 1:3). By sending Malachi to repeat the same message God shows his heart.

Here is the first powerful incentive to repent and return to God. He is a constant God. His gracious purposes do not change. Jesus Christ is the same yesterday, today and for ever (Hebrews 13:8). 'God has remained the same,' Malachi is saying. 'It is *you* who have changed; it is *you* who need to come back in repentance.'

2. *God is moved*
Here is the second incentive to return. God is not a heartless, severe potentate, who coldly hands out a grudging pardon to repentant people. Rather, when he sees people moving towards him, he moves lovingly towards them. 'Return to me and I will return to you,' says God. In other words, the people's return would find a ready and warm

response in God. He would return to them. These are wonderful words. The good news about God is that he is like the father in Jesus' parable of the prodigal son. As the young offender begins his journey of return. Jesus tells us, 'But while he was still a long way off, his father saw him and was filled with compassion; he ran to his son, threw his arms around him and kissed him.' Later we read of a great feast of celebration, with music and dancing, to rejoice at the prodigal's return. God is that kind of character. He is generous and fulsome in his pardon to repentant people. He delights in their return.

'Return to me and I will return to you,' says the Lord Almighty (3:7). This is a tremendous and gracious promise to any backslider. Many of us have fallen many times in our Christian walk. Sometimes there have been long periods of coldness of heart towards God. This is nothing to be proud of. But no matter how many times we fall, when we come seeking God again sincerely, he is more than willing to receive us back. This truth should not cause us to presume upon his love, but it should cause us to marvel at his loving-kindness. All too often these days, we come across people whose marriages have run into trouble. Sometimes there has been selfishness and neglect of one partner by the other. Sometimes there has been adultery. Perhaps realizing the dreadful mistake and wrong he or she has committed, the wayward partner returns penitently, asking, 'Will you take me back?' Sometimes the answer is 'yes'; sometimes the answer is 'no'. Sometimes people have just been hurt too much and feel they cannot face any more. But here is God, always ready to take us back as we come in honest repentance. God is always willing to heal our marriage to him. Hasn't he said that he hates divorce? (2:16.)

Perhaps you have made a profession of faith some time ago. But then your faith has drifted and you have got mixed up in the world, or you have set your heart on uncertain riches so that they have become your god. Perhaps, like the people of Malachi's day, you are a religious backslider. You have always kept up the outward form of worship, but in all honesty your heart has become bitter and cold. 'Return to me and I will return to you,' says the Lord Jesus Christ. That is a lovely promise!

The people of Malachi's day were so hard in their self-righteousness that there was no possibility of their returning to God until they were deeply convicted of their sin. Their attitudes were so hard that they would not easily admit that they had done anything wrong. So, having assured them of his constancy, God now addresses one of the chief matters over which they need to repent. Practically speaking, 'How are we to return?' God answers them.

A robbery (3:8,9)

The Lord charges his people with robbery. They have stolen from God. They have robbed God with respect to their tithes — the practice of giving a tenth of their income to God. They have robbed God in their offerings — voluntary gifts for special purposes over and above the tithe. **'Will a man rob God? Yet you rob me,'** says God. We will consider three questions concerning this charge of robbery.

1. *Is it really possible to rob God?*
Since all creation belongs to God, whether money remains in your pocket or goes into the offertory box in one sense is irrelevant; it all still belongs to God. But there is another sense in which God can be robbed.

Although the money which remains in your pocket ultimately still belongs to God, it cannot be used for his worship or to further the cause of God and truth in the world. To that extent you are robbing his work of the support which you ought to be giving it. Now in his sovereignty God is no doubt able to make up for what you have not given, but nevertheless you are robbing him of your support for his worship and the work of the gospel.

In this sense then giving money to the church or to missionary work or to Christian relief societies or directly to the poor is counted by God as giving to him. This is particularly brought out here in Malachi. The tithes of the

Old Testament Jews went to support the priests and Levites.
But at this period in the history of the Jews, the priests and
Levites were a pretty bad bunch. In one way we can understand people not wanting to give their money to them. But
even giving to the support of these priests, who were not
the people they ought to have been, was looked upon by
God as giving to him.

The second reason why it is possible to rob God is because
what we give of our money is a true indication of our genuine
heart devotion to God, and God is interested in our hearts.
The way we use our money tells us so much about ourselves.
I read recently of someone who was writing a biography of
the Duke of Wellington, the great victor at Waterloo. The
biographer discovered some old cheque stubs belonging to
the Duke. 'When I saw how he spent his money,' he said,
'I knew the man.' That's true, isn't it? Our hobbies, our
personal pleasures, our needs, the kind of things we really
value — it's all there to be read in the cheque book. Do
our cheque stubs speak of Jesus and our love to him? It is
the heart God is most interested in, and failure to use our
money for God speaks of a cold heart towards God. It
speaks of God robbed of devotion.

2. *How do Christians rob God?*
Let us be very practical and focus in on two obvious areas.

Firstly, the general idea of the tithe, although it finds
its origins in the Old Testament, is a right idea. We can
rob God by not tithing our possessions and our earnings.
We rob God, not by giving him nothing, but by giving him
less than we ought to (3:10). 'But', perhaps you say, 'we
can't have tithing; that is going back to the Mosaic law and
we are not under the law' (Galatians 5:18). But I argue that
Abraham (who in the context particularly of Galatians was
the man who received the promise of the gospel) was giving
tithes 430 years before the law existed (Genesis 14:20).
The law simply institutionalized what Abraham did willingly.
The gospel should free us from bondage to self to follow in
Abraham's footsteps out of love for God who first loved us.

But we should go beyond that. Jesus calls us to be those

whose righteousness exceeds that of the scribes and Pharisees, and those fastidious religionists were red-hot tithers! The tenth of everything they could think of, they gave! The tenth might be a good rule of thumb for the Christian, but if we stick to that legalistically in a way we are missing the point. The Christian is not ruled by the giving of a tenth; the Christian is to give *sacrificially*. Surely that is the governing factor. 'Therefore, I urge you, brothers, in view of God's mercy, to offer your bodies as living sacrifices, holy and pleasing to God — which is your spiritual worship' (Romans 12:1). Christ has sacrificed his life for us and we are to respond with sacrifice. You see, it may be possible for some wealthy Christians to rob God even though they give the tithe. If a tenth of our income is not a sacrifice then we are robbing God. We should give to God in such a way that we feel the pinch.

Secondly, the Jews of the Old Testament were called to give to God out of their earnings and their crops and their precious things. We live in a very different time and culture from ancient Israel. In a changing world there are perhaps things which have become even more precious than money. Ancient Israel had an agricultural economy where life was slow and peaceful. We live in a world which seems always to be travelling at a million miles an hour! Very often our most precious commodity is our *time*. I heard a Christian speaker recently at a family conference who said that often the best way for a husband to let his wife know that he really loves her is to go and waste time with her, shopping or something. Time has become so precious that if you are prepared to 'waste' time with another person, that person must be a top priority with you! We can rob God by trying to keep time mostly to ourselves — time that should be given to God in personal prayer; time that should be given to God in family praise and worship; time that should be given to God in serving the needs of the local expression of the body of Christ. Are we robbing God? This does not mean that we are to have no time for relaxation or for our families. That would be quite wrong. But is time for God and the needs of his kingdom a definite part of our busy schedule?

Perhaps even more pertinent than our time is our *concentration*. Our jobs today require so much effort and careful thought. The detailed thinking and energy which some people put into their hobby is amazing. The prodigious hours of practice given to the musical instrument by the budding musician in order to master the skill is a great feat of human endeavour. We are left asking, though, 'What level of concentration do we give to the things of God?' The continuing work of making God's Word come with freshness and power to the twentieth century needs a concentrated effort.

But robbing God brings a penalty upon the robbers. We cannot rob God with impunity. **'You are under a curse — the whole nation of you — because you are robbing me'** (3:9). From looking at verses 10–12 it is plain that for the nation of Malachi's time this meant that God had sent meagre harvests, and diseases and insect pests upon their crops. As part of their punishment for robbing God, Israel was being despised by others as the poor relation among the community nations. This leads us to a third question about robbing God.

3. *How are the robbers cursed today?*
Old Testament Israel tilled the promised land, sowed seed and lived by the crop. But the church lives by sowing a different kind of seed and looking for a different kind of crop. We sow the Word of God in the gospel and we look for a harvest of conversions. The penalty for robbing God today, as with Old Testament Israel, is often that our harvests are blighted. When our love to God is so meagre that we fail to put our hands into our pockets then the Holy Spirit withdraws from such a church. The Word is preached, but there is little or no accompanying conviction and saving activity of the Holy Spirit. Have you ever been in a church where for months and months and months there have been no conversions? It is like visiting a barren land, where the harvest has been cursed. Look at it another way. If this group of Christians has so little genuine love for God that they are skimping as much as possible on their offerings

to him, that is hardly the kind of fellowship into which God will feel able to introduce new converts. How can such a fellowship with such little regard for God be entrusted with helping in the development of a new babe in Christ?

When God's people will not give to the support of God's work, it has a very direct and practical effect upon their influence. Perhaps a pastor is not well supported. He is forever worried about the financial needs of his family. You cannot expect a man who is continually plagued by such anxieties to produce the best sermons and teaching from God's Word. Perhaps the church meets in a tumble-down old building much in need of renovation, but because of the lack of financial support, or willingness to give time and effort to a working party, it remains in a state of dis-repair. All right. But outsiders are put off from entering such a building to hear the gospel. They are not attracted into the building. So the influence of the church declines. We cannot rob God without hurting ourselves. He wants us to give to him.

There is a more long-term way in which robbing God affects us. As Christians we have the great privilege and possibility of storing up treasure in heaven. Now that doesn't mean that we can have our account at Barclays literally transferred to the bank of heaven. Jesus is not speaking of literal money when he speaks of this. But look at it this way. Other things on which we spend our money are all part of this passing world. One day this world and everything in it will all be gone. However, when the world has gone, nevertheless all that has been accomplished for God in this world will remain for eternity. Victories won for Christ, times when Christians have been encouraged in the faith, folk who have been converted — these things will stand for ever. One day we will stand in heaven and ask ourselves what we did with our money. Did we invest it in that which facilitates God's work and which stands for ever? Or did we fritter it away on a bad investment in this passing world? Robbing God we rob ourselves.

As we see, then, the return which God had in mind for Malachi's contemporaries was a very practical repentance, concerning their tithes and offerings. True repentance always does come down to very practical matters. In New Testament times the church at Ephesus had lost their first love. What was the divine remedy? 'Repent and *do* the things you did at first' (Revelation 2:5). Love for God is not love for him at all unless it expresses itself in a practical way.

A reward (3:10–12)

God looks for practical repentance. But he is a gracious and loving God. So the next thing we read of is a tender and generous incentive from the Lord for the nation to return. ' "Bring the whole tithe into the storehouse, that there may be food in my house. Test me in this," says the Lord Almighty, "and see if I will not throw open the floodgates of heaven and pour out so much blessing that you will not have room enough for it" ' (3:10).

In verses 10–12 the Lord promises that four marvellous blessings will flow to them from a whole-hearted obedience.

1. *Abundance*
God promises to supply all their needs abundantly. The floodgates of heaven will be thrown open (3:10). They will not know where to store such a bumper harvest. God is promising a blessing totally out of proportion to what their repentance deserved. We see the incredible generosity of God.

2. *Protection*
Sometimes it was possible for the blessings of a great harvest to be lost or snatched away because of pests and plant diseases. But God promises, 'I will prevent pests from devouring your crops, and the vines in your fields will not cast their fruit' (3:11). So often it can look as if blessing is about to come, only for it to be lost at the last moment. But here God is promising a blessing which cannot be snatched away. It will be a blessing which is secure and which they can enjoy to the full.

3. *Reputation*

As they repent and sincerely return to God with all their hearts, God's blessing will bring a vast reputation to them among the other nations. ' "Then all the nations will call you blessed, for yours will be a delightful land," says the Lord Almighty' 3:12). The reputation of the Jewish nation was at a low ebb. Many times they had gone about seeking to re-establish a reputation for themselves. But God tells them to concentrate on serving him and *he* will build their reputation in the eyes of others.

4. *Certainty*

To be obedient to God whole-heartedly and unreservedly can appear to be a very risky business to those who do not know God. It can appear that you are chancing your life's good on a very long shot. But God challenges the people of Judah: 'Test me!' 'Prove me in this . . .' The Jews were not well off at the time. To give all the tithes would indeed involve some real sacrifice and hardship. On the surface it might well seem that if they gave these things to God they would not have enough food for themselves to see them through the year to the next harvest. It seemed a risk. But if they had the faith to step out on the promise of God and put themselves in this seemingly exposed position then God would respond miraculously. They would have the overwhelming joy of seeing him intervene on their behalf. Any lingering doubts they had about God and his power and his love would be expelled. They would see God's response and conclude, 'Well, he really is there! He truly does keep his word! Once we had a second-hand faith we had learned from previous generations; now we have seen God at work for ourselves!' All this would be a blessing in and of itself. It would bring assurance and certainty to their walk with God.

Can we now see what is going on in this passage of Malachi? God's call to obedience was really a call to exercise faith in him. And it is faith which opens the windows of heaven.

Often we can restrict our 'obedience' as Christians to a

life-style which involves no 'risks', no faith in God. Our Christian walk is reduced to something which is virtually indistinguishable from mere 'respectability' plus church attendance. The floodgates of heaven remain firmly closed and the church remains powerless and without reputation.

But here we are called to the exercise of practical faith in God. The repentance God calls for leads to faith. We are called to go out on a limb on his promises and trust him.

Spurgeon, who saw such a fruitful ministry, said this to his students preparing for the ministry: 'It is proven by all observation that success in the Lord's service is very generally in proportion to faith. It is certainly not in proportion to ability, nor does it always run parallel to a display of zeal; but it is invariably according to the measure of faith, for this is a law of the kingdom without exception, "According to your faith be it unto you." '[16]

How can we see the blessing of God? How can we see the cause of Christ making headway? If you are asking such questions, then the word of Jesus to you is the word he gave to a father longing to see his child freed from the bondage of the devil's snares: 'Everything is possible for him who believes' (Mark 9:23).

Were the floodgates of heaven ever opened upon the Jews in such a way that they had no room to contain the blessing?

Perhaps we should see that Malachi's promise had to wait its fulfilment until a group of Jews, whole-heartedly seeking to be obedient to God and believing the promise of the Father, gathered in an upper room in Jerusalem for constant prayer. The last time the windows of heaven had been opened was at the judgement in Noah's flood. But on the Day of Pentecost the Holy Spirit was poured out from heaven upon the Jews in such an almighty way that the blessing flooded out to the whole world and continues even to this very day to bring forth an abundant harvest for God.

Be assured — God never leaves true faith unrewarded!

10.
Two kinds of talk

Please read Malachi 3:13—18

The first page of our Bible tells us that God spoke and in speaking created the world. There is a sense in which we create a world verbally. Our words affect others — our family, our friends, even ourselves — and create a world, an atmosphere in which we live. Our words can create a world of encouragement and relaxation. The things we say can create an atmosphere of tension or despair.

In this section Malachi turns to the subject of the things people say. Throughout his book, as we have already noted, Malachi has a very distinctive method of getting his message over. We might call it 'the disputation method'. He makes a positive charge against his hearers. Then he gives the kind of response he expects from his hearers. This is usually a question which feigns total ignorance and innocence of Malachi's charge and in fact reflects the spiritual deadness and arrogance of the people. Then Malachi comes in again in more detail and nails them down! (1:2; 1:6,7; 2:17; 3:7,8.) We have come to the last of these question-and-answer disputations and it introduces a section which tells us about using the power of the tongue for evil or for good.

Harsh talk (3:13—15)

' "You have said harsh things against me," says the Lord. "Yet you ask, 'What have we said against you?' You have said, 'It is futile to serve God' " ' (3:13,14).

111

Here are harsh, hard words against God. We will ask four simple questions about them.

1. *What kind of talk is this exactly?*
Sometimes the dealings of God with his people are difficult to understand. At such times some Christians quote to us 'All things work together for good . . .' in a shallow and almost heartless way which has very little feeling for those who are experiencing trouble. People who have served the Lord faithfully and lovingly are not exempt from calamities. At such times of crisis God expects us to be honest with him and to come and pour out our agonies and our disappointments humbly to him. Not to do so is to be less than real with God. We are brought low and we stand sometimes speechless before the mystery of his providence. But in faith we reserve judgement on what God has allowed to happen. Only he knows the end from the beginning. He is God and we are human beings.

However, in Malachi's time there were people who, under a pretence of being 'honest', were taking it upon themselves to jump to conclusions about God and his ways. They felt themselves to be the epitome of godliness. How dare God allow trouble to enter their lives? Their immediate response to the first hint of trouble was 'It is futile to serve God. What did we gain from carrying out his requirements?' (3:14.) Their talk said that God did not keep his promises. It slandered God's name. It said he was unjust. 'What did we gain by . . . going about like mourners before the Lord Almighty?' (3:14.) There are some things which are inappropriate for a funeral. At a funeral the mourners are careful to be on their best behaviour. But these people were saying that they saw no point in being careful about serving God.

This is faithless talk. It is talk which arrogantly points the finger at God (though these people thought other people arrogant, 3:15). It is self-righteous talk (it is other people who are the evil-doers, 3:15). It is also talk which discourages others from serving God. It makes people who hear it feel that there is no point in serving the Lord, that they might as well give up. So spiritually it is very dangerous indeed.

2. *When was this talk uttered?*
Well, it might have been spoken in open conversation, but in Israel, God's chosen people, where it was the respectable thing to honour God, it was probably not uttered openly. These harsh sentiments against the Lord may have been expressed during private conversation. Perhaps they were words spoken last thing at night between husband and wife. Perhaps they were words said under the breath. Perhaps they might have been simply thoughts which were nurtured in the mind and never spoken audibly.

But, whether public or private, expressed or unexpressed, God heard them. Also it is quite extraordinary how even attitudes which we never speak about can communicate themselves to others. There is such a thing as 'body language'. Actions not only speak louder than words, but often make plain things about which a person has remained silent. So the cancer of harsh and discouraging sentiments can spread among the people of God.

3. *Where do we find such talk today?*
Obviously we would expect to find it in the comments on Christianity from the world around us. 'It is a waste of time using your Sundays like that. You would be better off having a lie in! How foolish to serve God!'

But we are looking at Malachi preaching to Judah and he was finding this kind of talk among the professed people of God. So do we, and it comes at us from many different directions and at many different levels. Let me suggest a few areas.

a. Liberal theology. The ecclesiastical dignitaries who hold high office often tell us that 'The Bible is a great servant but a terrible master.' They discourage people from taking God's Word seriously. The virgin birth, the bodily resurrection of Jesus and even the deity of Christ are denied. I once saw a copy of *The Myth of God Incarnate* on sale in an Islamic

bookshop! At root this is a contradiction of God's statements and God's promises. It is implied that Christian
salvation is not actually as good as we were naively led to
believe. It is almost as if God could not possibly make it
that good as to give us true bodily eternal life of which
Jesus' resurrection is the proof. God could not be that
good, as to come for us in the flesh and die for us. This
is harsh talk against God, which discourages faith.

b. Cynicism. The dictionary defines a cynic as a person
who sarcastically doubts human sincerity and merit. Nothing
is ever done with good intention. Nothing is ever as good as
it could be. Things will always turn out badly.

There are people like that in churches. When anything
goes wrong their words come flowing out: 'I told you so!'
'What did you expect!' Often the cynic hides his remark
behind dry humour. In a humorous book I came across
'Chisholm's First Law of Human Interaction'.[17] It is this:
'If anything can possibly go wrong – it will.' And the law
has a corollary. 'If anything just can't go wrong – it will
anyway.' We can smile at such quips. But too much of
that kind of talk betrays more than a playful sense of
humour. From Christians it can be tantamount to accusing
God of always letting us down.

c. Materialism. Living in our materialistic culture and often
being confronted with the apparent happiness and comfort
of the ungodly we can very easily fall into the temptation
of Asaph in Psalm 73: 'I envied the arrogant when I saw
the prosperity of the wicked. They have no struggles . . .
They are free from the burdens common to man.' 'Oh, to
be rich and have an easy life! Oh, the hardship of this
Christian life!' Our feet can quickly slip into living for
personal comfort rather than for God and his glory, even
while still attending church. But basically that reveals an
attitude which repeats the words of the people of Malachi's
day: 'It is futile to serve God.' The true state of people
who are 'Christians' and 'serving God' for what they hope

to get out of him, rather than because they honestly love him, is exposed in this attitude.

d. The 'if only . . .' syndrome. There are some folk within church circles who give one the impression that they spend a lot of time thinking like this: 'I've been serving God all these years, and look where it has got me. If only I had . . .' People who go through life with this 'if only . . .' attitude are harming themselves spiritually. Instead of trusting the sovereign God to do what is right they virtually accuse him of wasting their lives for them. The 'if only . . .' outlook is dangerous. It is like driving a car with your eye exclusively taken up with what is in the rear-view mirror. That is the way to head for a crash.

These things, and many more, are examples of today's harsh talk against the Lord.

4. *How do people come to talk like this?*
Beneath a religious veneer, the contemporaries of Malachi were making vicious insinuations against God. This was a very serious sin and we need to have some idea of how these people came into this bitter state, lest we fall into it ourselves. The source of their problem seems to be that they had forgotten two things.

Firstly, people can start talking like this when they forget to see *the present in the light of the future judgement of God.* The apostle Paul was being totally accurate when he said that, 'If only for this life we have hope in Christ, we are to be pitied more than all men' (1 Corinthians 15:19). You see, for Paul faith in Christ was never contemplated as a royal route to material prosperity, health and ease. Rather Christianity had brought Paul trouble, persecution and hardship, along with the joy of knowing Christ. Compared to other folk in the world, the Christians of Paul's day were to be pitied if this life is all. If we forget the future, therefore, it is very easy to slip into accusing God.

But one of the great themes of the Bible is that this life is not all. There is a world to come. There is to be a judgement. There is an eternal heaven and an eternal hell. There

is to be a separation of the righteous and the wicked, as
Malachi reminds his hearers in verses 17 and 18 of our
section. At the beginning of chapter 4, Malachi brings power-
fully before the people the fact that **'Surely the day is
coming; it will burn like a furnace'** (4:1). In Psalm 73 Asaph
was tempted to envy the wicked and so implicitly accuse
God, until he understood their final destiny, that suddenly
they will be 'completely swept away by terrors' (Psalm
73:17,19). Sometimes the apostle Paul found the Christian
life hard, but in the light of eternity he saw it very
differently: 'I consider that our present sufferings are not
worth comparing with the glory that will be revealed in us'
(Romans 8:18).

The athlete who runs well is the one who concentrates
all his attention on the finishing tape and is not distracted
by the crowd. The antidote to harsh thoughts against God
is to think of the future. Always bear in mind what he has
saved us from and what he has saved us to. John Wesley
said, 'I desire to have both heaven and hell ever in my eye,
while I stand on this isthmus of life, between these two
boundless oceans: and I verily think the daily consideration
of both highly becomes all men of reason and religion.'

Secondly people can start talking harshly against God
when they have forgotten *the dangers of partial obedience*.
One of the biggest problems facing Malachi as he tried to
bring these people back to God was the fact that they
thought that they had been giving themselves to God. 'Look,
Malachi, we have served God and he has given us no blessing.
It has been a waste of time to serve him.' But if we look
back over what Malachi has said to them, for example about
their sacrifices and their tithing, God's argument with them
was not that they had given him no service, but that it had
been only partial service. Outwardly they had kept up the
temple services, but where were their hearts? They had
brought some offerings, but where was the *whole* tithe?
(3:10.)

The fact that it was only partial obedience was the reason
why God did not bless them. They nodded in God's direction,

but that was all. In fact they treated God as an also-ran. They never put him first. They wanted to serve God *and* self.

Do you see the dangers of partial obedience? God cannot bless it, but at the same time it gives the sinful heart the excuse to say, 'But we have served God.' Satan's ploy of partial obedience is a very clever trap. Partial obedience is an enormously dangerous matter. It can twist itself around and lend fuel to all the accusations against God. It can lead people into a deep pit of bitterness and vehemence against God. Sincere and whole-hearted devotion to God is the only safe road.

Forgetting the future and partial obedience were the roots of this wicked discouraging harsh talk against God. But as godly people in Judah heard these words against God they felt they must do something to shield themselves from it. They sat down and decided to act. Perhaps some who had slipped into harsh talk themselves took Malachi's rebuke, repented and sought to change. Repentance calls for change at the very point of sin. So the next few verses of Malachi's book introduce us to a different style of speech.

Honourable talk (3:16—18)

Some people realized that if they went on much longer in this climate of conversation, where all they heard poured scorn on God, then very soon they too would end up bitter and faithless. Their response was to seek each other out and to talk together.

'Then those who feared the Lord talked with each other, and the Lord listened and heard' (3:16).

One person said to himself, 'Now that person there seems to fear God. I'm going to invite him round and we are going to talk together, not about the cost of living, nor the first division championship, nor the weather, but we are going to share together about our mutual fear and regard for God.'

They did not just listen to God's Word together, but they spoke together about it. In your church after the sermon what is the conversation about? It would be unnatural and false if that conversation never included day-to-day affairs concerning folk's well-being and the events of life. But if, as can often be the case, the things of God are hardly ever mentioned in that conversation, then something is wrong. God and his ways should be part and parcel of our everyday conversation. This is what God had impressed upon the Jewish people from the beginning. 'These commandments that I give you today are to be upon your hearts . . . Talk about them when you sit at home and when you walk along the road, when you lie down and when you get up' (Deuteronomy 6:6,7). The godly few of Malachi's time were seeking to take that seriously. When 'religious talk' is reserved for Sunday or kept in that little box of time marked 'family worship', then religion becomes very unreal and awkward. But those who really feared the Lord wanted him in all their lives. So they engaged together in conversation which 'honoured his name' (3:16).

God's name is honoured when we speak the truth about him. He is not honoured by lies or by fanciful theories about him. He is honoured by the truth. When people are going through the mill, to bring the words of Scripture tenderly to them is often of great benefit. The person may already know the particular words of the Bible, but it can be a real help just to hear those words from the lips of someone else who truly believes them.

The truth about God from our own experience is good to share with others at the appropriate time. Having been battered by the harsh, cynical words which Malachi has outlined, there must have been many bewildered souls for whom God stood in the dock. The devil, using the faithless words of others, may well have people in doubt and questioning, 'Is God faithful? Does God care?' The Lord is on trial. At such a time for someone to get up into the witness box, as it were, and explain from his own experience how the Lord helped him in a certain situation can be a great help and can rekindle a dying faith.

Their conversation promoted the fear and honour of God. We do not fear someone who is irrelevant, or dead, or absent. Their conversation was not just of bald detached doctrine. It concerned the truths and doctrines of God, but in such a way that it left people feeling, 'God is someone to be reckoned with now — today!' It left people realizing that he is the living God. It stirred them up to look to him and to expect him to be at work among *them*. It moved them to worship him from their hearts.

At the time of the nativity of Christ we are told that there was an informal group of people who were 'looking forward to the redemption of Jerusalem'. Anna the prophetess and old Simeon were a part of that group where faith was alive and yearning for God to come. They seemed to be a group who shared among themselves, and no doubt with all who would listen, the truths of God and their hopes for the future. These people seem very much to be the spiritual descendants of those who in Malachi's time spoke together to the honour of God.

Unlike the vicious and discouraging words which Malachi exposed at the beginning of this section, this talk, which honoured God and proclaimed his faithfulness, relevance and goodness, would have created an environment of mutually building faith. These 'honourable talkers', not the 'harsh-talkers', are to be our pattern for speech. 'Do not let any unwholesome talk come out of your mouths, but only what is helpful for building others up according to their needs, that it may benefit those who listen' (Ephesians 4:29).

Malachi goes on to tell us the Lord's reaction as he heard this honourable and encouraging conversation: '. . . and the Lord listened and heard. A scroll of remembrance was written in his presence concerning those who feared the Lord and honoured his name. "They will be mine," says the Lord Almighty, "in the day when I make up my treasured possession. I will spare them, just as in compassion a man spares his son who serves him. And you will again see the distinction between the righteous and the wicked, between those who serve God and those who do not" ' (3:16—18).

There is divine recognition and delight in the conversation of those who feared God. These people were taking practical steps to honour God and to strengthen their faith. They were seeking to help one another renew their faith and love for God. It was that which the Lord listened to and heard.

The scroll of remembrance which was made up before God was not a list of good deeds. Rather it was a book of the names of those who feared and honoured God. Their practical seeking to honour God and to encourage each other's trust in the Lord showed that they had true faith and their names were entered into the Lamb's book of life. There their names are contemplated by God himself and never forgotten. What tremendous encouragement Malachi was now bringing to this little group of faithful people! The cynical time-serving priests probably despised them. But Malachi relates to them that God says of them, 'They will be mine.' They are God's crown jewels, the pride of the Lord's treasury. They are his sons (3:17). 'They will be mine'. We see here an expression of determination in the Lord's love for his people. They *will* be his. He is determined to have them in heaven and nothing will stop him. That determination was such that Jesus went all the way to the cross for his people. His love was such that no price was too high for him to pay. What love!

Malachi is relating to these faithful few how much the Lord loves them. On the coming Day of Judgement these will be distinguished from the wicked (3:18). They will be saved. They will be spared. They will be given preferential treatment. Earlier in this section we saw how the bitter harsh-talking religionists were accusing God and saying that he makes no distinction between the righteous and the wicked (3:14). Now God is answering them and telling them that the Day of Judgement is coming when he will make the distinction.

But in fact the distinction is apparent already, isn't it? It is not between material well-being and poverty. That is not the way the righteous and the wicked are already distinguished. Nor is it a distinction between easy comfortable lives and troublesome lives. But the distinction between the righteous and the wicked is already apparent in the two kinds of talk. The distinction of judgement day is already seen in those who are talking honourably of God and taking practical steps to encourage their faith and those who are not. Of course! Didn't our Lord say, 'No good tree bears bad fruit, not does a bad tree bear good fruit . . . The good man brings good things out of the good stored up in his heart, and the evil man brings evil things out of the evil stored up in his heart. For out of the overflow of his heart his mouth speaks'? (Luke 6:43—45.)

This paragraph leaves us with a challenge. The reason is that there is a single thought underlying this section. The two kinds of talk are in fact one kind of talk. They are both overheard by God. God listens to all we say. That fact underlies all that Malachi says here. The Lord misses nothing. He knew the bitter words of some. He knew what those who truly feared him were saying. God knows all our words. That is why gossip and back-stabbing are ultimately pointless and fearfully sinful.

The great theologian Augustine had a notice written up on his dining room wall. It said this: 'He is unwelcome at this table who speaks an unkind word against an absent brother.'

Jesus said, 'But I tell you that men will have to give account on the day of judgement for every careless word they have spoken. For by your words you will be acquitted, and by your words you will be condemned' (Matthew 12:36,37).

11.
The day of the Lord

Please read Malachi 4:1—6

This final section of the prophecy of Malachi speaks of 'the day of the Lord' (4:1,3,5). The biblical view of history is not cyclical, it is linear. It has a definite beginning, with God's creation of the universe, and it is building to a final climax. In the present world there is much sin, unfairness and inequality, but the terminus of history is the great Day of Judgement on which the scales of justice will ultimately be balanced. God is waiting. Man is allowed to do his worst. But the day of the Lord is coming and Malachi tells us that we are to view everything in the light of that coming day.

In Scripture, the phrase 'the day of the Lord' refers primarily, though not exclusively, to the return of Jesus Christ. Throughout history, through wars, famines and in other ways, God carries out temporal judgements upon the nations. But these 'days of the Lord' merely foreshadow 'the great and dreadful day of the Lord' (4:5), when Christ returns, the dead are raised, heaven and earth as we know them pass away, making way for the new heaven and earth, and God's final judgement is executed. Malachi begins his last comments to us by giving something of a description of that last day.

A picture of the last day (4:1—3)

The central feature of this picture is the sun (4:2). Malachi reminds us that the rising of the same sun can bring about two very different effects.

122

Imagine the brilliant blue sky and radiant sunshine which you might have seen on a Near East travel brochure. It is an agricultural setting. It is early morning. The summer months have come. There has been no rain for weeks and the land is tinder dry. The sun climbs above the horizon and begins to burn down with terrible heat upon the stubble in the fields. The day 'burns like a furnace' (4:1). It becomes unbearably hot. Then, as the intensity of the heat increases, perhaps the sun's rays are focused by reflecting off some distant object and, quite suddenly, the parched vegetation catches fire, blazes up and soon the fields as far as the eye can see have been ignited. Sparks are carried, smoke billows and the fire spreads uncontrollably, destroying everything in its path. The rising of the sun that day has brought awful destruction.

But now, some miles down the road, we have a different scene. There are some young calves that have been cooped up in a dirty, old, smelly, dark shed for weeks on end. It seems as if the farmer has forgotten about them. They have had no freedom. They are ailing and restless under their confinement. But on that day the farmer lets them out for the first time into the sun and it is marvellous (4:2). They feel the lovely warmth of the sun upon their backs, they bask in the warm air and it is not long before they are running and leaping for joy over the ashes of the burnt-out fields (4:3). For these animals it is a day of release and healing and joyous refreshment.

The same sun has brought two very different effects. To some it has brought delight; to others it has brought utter destruction. This is Malachi's picture of the Day of Judgement. Let us fill in the details.

The sun is not the star at the centre of our planetary system, but it is the 'sun of righteousness' (4:2). This is the Lord Jesus Christ. He comes, not shining with electro-magnetic radiation, but rather radiating righteousness. He comes to usher in 'a new heaven and a new earth, the home of righteousness' (2 Peter 3:13). The 'wings' of the sun (4:2) probably refer to the sun's rays.

The stubble is identified as 'all the arrogant and every

evildoer' (4:1). The sun of righteousness will destroy them 'root and branch' (4:1). This is not teaching a judgement of annihilation, where the wicked simply cease to exist. The Bible does not teach that. The destruction such that 'not a root or a branch will be left to them' refers to the fact that there will be no second chance on the Day of Judgement. There is no root left to start afresh. There is no branch or shoot that can be grafted on somewhere else to make a new beginning. The judgement is final and irreversible.

The calves (4:2) are not perfect people, but they are people who honestly revere God's name. They are failing sinners, but sinners who sincerely have an affection for the Lord. On that day when the sun of righteousness bursts into the blue, they will know release and joy and happiness such as they have never known. They will know this because, although they are failing sinners, yet nevertheless they have experienced the salvation of God, who has given them a new heart which hates and grieves over sin and which loves righteousness. Probably the greatest source of their sorrows in this life is grief over sin and its effects. They honestly wish that they never sinned. When the Lord Jesus comes, and they witness the final defeat of all sin and evil, that will be a day of celebration, of gladness and rejoicing. They will 'trample down the wicked under the soles of [their] feet' (4:3). They will 'leap like calves released from the stall'. Vexed by the injustice in the world and the remaining sin in their own lives they will find that 'the sun of righteousness will rise with healing in its wings'.

As we have seen in the previous section, there were those in Malachi's time who were questioning whether or not it was worthwhile to serve God (3:14). Is it worthwhile to be a Christian, to take up the cross and engage in a lifelong struggle with sin, which can seem so restrictive and such a narrow path? Malachi teaches that in the light of the last day, it is profoundly worthwhile.

But if we see what Malachi is saying in this obvious sense alone, we are missing the searching thrust of his words. We must ponder again, 'To whom is this warning concerning the day of the Lord addressed?' To whom was God speaking when he warned of this day? Is it addressed to the world which blatantly rejects God and his Word? No. Doubtless the world needs to take heed, for they will be judged on that day, but Malachi's warning is not primarily for them. It is addressed to Judah, to the descendants of Jacob, to the professed people of God.

The dreadful truth is that not only are there two kinds of people on earth — the saved and the lost — but there are two kinds of people within the professed church — the saved and the lost. The awful truth is that when Christ returns, he will come not only to judge the world, but also to judge the professed church. There were two kinds of people within Judah. There were those who gave God insincere worship with blemished, cheap 'sacrifices', and there were those who did their best honestly to revere God's name because they loved him. Malachi is telling us that Jesus will return to judge between us all.

Reading the words of Jesus in the Gospels, we find that he repeatedly warns us that on the Day of Judgement there *will* be many people who are expecting to be welcomed into heaven but who in fact will be cast out into hell. These people thought they were Christians, but actually they never belonged to the Lord and their heartless, careless service of him showed it.

Think of Jesus telling the parable of the ten virgins. All ten of them were waiting for the bridegroom (Matthew 25:1–12). 'At that time the kingdom of heaven will be like ten virgins who took their lamps and went out to meet the bridegroom.' All ten of them were looking forward to entering into the wedding celebration. But half of them had made no proper preparations; they had not brought enough oil to keep their lamps burning, and one cannot help feeling that their careless, sloppy approach to their duty reflected a lack of real devotion to the bridegroom. When it was too late, they went to buy oil, but returned to find themselves locked out from the celebrations. Many will foolishly look forward to heaven who will never enter heaven because, for all their religion, they never had faith and love for Jesus.

Jesus closes his parable with the shocking spectacle of the bridegroom refusing them entry and saying to them the most terrible words: 'I tell you the truth, I don't know you' (Matthew 25:12).

Similar startling words come from our Lord's mouth in the Sermon on the Mount: 'Not everyone who says to me, "Lord, Lord", will enter the kingdom of heaven, but only he who does the will of my Father who is in heaven. Many will say to me on that day, "Lord, Lord, did we not prophesy in your name, and in your name drive out demons and perform many miracles?" Then I will tell them plainly, "I never knew you. Away from me, you evildoers!' (Matthew 7:21–23.) Here are people who profess Jesus as Lord, yet are lost, because it was only a profession. It was only empty words. There was never a real love affair between Christ and their souls.

The awesome solemnity of what Jesus is teaching here and in other places is driven home by the fact that the verdict of the last day is final. Once it has been pronounced it will never be revoked. This hit me with renewed vigour several years ago while I was visiting a friend's house. I listened to a recording of an old preacher delivering a mighty sermon on the subject of hell. The speaker was taking his hearers on a tour of hell. He explained how he imagined that if we were able to travel on this tour of such prodigious gravity we would presently see a whole group of people weeping on their knees and beating on a door marked 'Exit'. They would be crying out in loud voices of desperation: 'Let us out, let us out!' 'But,' the old preacher went on to explain, 'the heartbreaking sadness of that picture is this. The door marked "Exit" is only in their minds. It exists only in their imagination, for in reality there is no exit from hell.' On the Day of Judgement eternal issues will be settled *for ever*. Who can describe, therefore, what it must be to hear the Saviour say, 'Depart from me; I never knew you'? We dare not risk our souls. We are among the professed church, but are we among the Lord's people? Our name appears on the list of church members, but does it appear in the Lamb's book of life?

God would bring this terrible truth of the Day of Judgement before people who are unmoved and happy to have religious duty devoid of true affection for the Son of God. Let me remind you again of the possibility of the phenomenon of the evangelical Pharisee. There is the whited sepulchre of sound doctrine and respectable living, but within there is the stench of no love for Jesus! 'All the arrogant and every evildoer will be stubble, and that day that is coming will set them on fire. Not a root or a branch will be left to them. But for you who revere my name, the sun of righteousness will rise with healing in its wings.' This is the warning.

But let us remember the gracious purpose of God in sending us these terrible warnings. Why does he warn us? Because he wants to wake people up to their danger that they might repent and be saved. Often the sternest and most terrifying warnings of God are the tokens of his deepest love. He warns us because he loves us and desires to save us. It may be one of the hardest things in the world for a person who has been a respected church member for many years to own up and confess that he has never actually experienced the new birth, and that in all honesty he has no experience of sins forgiven and therefore of true love for Jesus. But if that is the case, and someone has the guts and the integrity to own up to that, break his heart before God, tell him of his state and beg for forgiveness through the blood of Christ and ask for the Holy Spirit to truly flood his life, then he can be absolutely assured of the most loving welcome and reception from God. He warns us because he loves us.

When God sounds the alarm of judgement it is a blessed thing. How much more terrible to be left ignorant of the approaching day! That which we first hear as an alarm bell of judgement very often turns into the wedding bell of conversion to Christ!

John Angell James preached the gospel at Carrs Lane in Birmingham during the last century. He once told this story: 'How many has the prospect of a day of judgement alarmed in the midst of their sins; how many has it checked; how many has it been a means of converting! I knew a lady in high life, one of the most accomplished women I ever

met . . . one night she dreamed that the day of judgement
had arrived. She saw the Judge, in awful majesty, commence
the great assize. Around him, in a circle, the diameter of
which no eye could measure, were drawn the human race,
awaiting their doom. With slow and solemn pace, he
traversed the whole circle; whomsoever he approved, to them
he gave the token of his acceptance by graciously laying
his hand upon their heads. Many he passed, and gave them
no sign. As he approached the dreamer her anxiety to know
whether she should receive the token of his acceptance
became intense, till as he drew still nearer, and was about
to stop before her, the agony of her mind awoke her. It was
but a dream; a blessed one, however, for her. It produced
through the divine blessing, a deep solicitude for the
salvation of her soul. She became an eminent and devoted
Christian.'[18] The Lord's warnings of the last day are often
the tokens of his particular love. Oh, that those who are
warned may respond to God's affection!

The preparation for the last day (4:4—6)

In the last few verses of his book Malachi indicates to his
contemporaries the kind of life and attitudes that the Lord
longs to see among the people of Judah. The Lord in his
grace will send someone who will seek to prepare the nation
for the coming day.

Let us look at this section and first of all pick up the
historical details, then secondly draw out one final lesson.

What did God do in order to seek to prepare the Jews
and make them ready for that day? We are directed to
Moses and to John the Baptist.

'Remember the law of my servant Moses, the decrees
and laws I gave him at Horeb for all Israel' (4:4). The book
of Malachi began by reminding us of the covenant God had
made with Israel (1:2). These closing verses direct us again
to the covenant and to the obligations Israel was under to
fulfil its covenant responsibilities. Malachi points afresh to
the law of Moses. But how does the law help prepare people

for judgement day? It is very tempting to think that God is indicating to them that if they keep the law with all its commands then all will be well with them on the last day. But in fact, according to the New Testament, that is to misunderstand the purpose of the law. Fallen men and women can never perfectly keep the law. In his letter to the Galatian churches the apostle Paul gives the authoritative answer to the question: 'What, then, was the purpose of the law?' (Galatians 3:19). He proves from the Old Testament Scriptures that actually salvation has never been a matter of merit. Salvation can never be earned by good living and law-keeping. Salvation was and is and always will be a matter of God's free mercy. It is a gift which God gives to all who trust in Christ. The purpose of the law is not that people might merit salvation by law-keeping, but to alert people to the fact that they are sinners, that no matter how hard they try they cannot keep God's commandments for right living and that therefore they need a Saviour. We must believe that ultimately this was God's motive in directing the Jews of Malachi's day to the law, in order to prepare them for the last day. If they studied the law with honesty, they would see their sin and failure, and so cry out to God for mercy and trust the promised Saviour. 'The law was put in charge to lead us to Christ that we might be justified by faith' (Galatians 3:24).

Secondly, the Lord through Malachi speaks of Elijah. **'See, I will send you the prophet Elijah before that great and dreadful day of the Lord comes'** (4:5). Jesus' words, recorded in the Gospel of Matthew, make it clear that this verse has special reference to the ministry of John the Baptist (Matthew 11:14). John the Baptist preached the law of God, he cried for justice and purity and sincerity with all his heart and urged people tirelessly to own up to their sins and failures without trying to shift the blame or pretend they were better than they really were. He preached a baptism of repentance.

There is a very direct sense in which the ministry of John the Baptist, in preparing the nation for the ministry

of Jesus, prepared people for the day of the Lord. This is
because there is a sense in which the last day, the Day of
Judgement, was brought forward and broke into history
with the coming of Jesus. This can be traced in many ways
through the Gospels but verses like John 3:18—21 make it
plain. In the context of eternal judgement, Jesus says, speaking of himself, 'Whoever believes in him is not condemned,
but whoever does not believe *stands condemned already*
because he has not believed in the name of God's only
begotten Son. This is the verdict: Light has come into the
world, but men loved darkness instead of light because
their deeds were evil. Everyone who does evil hates the
light, and will not come into the light for fear that his deeds
will be exposed. But whoever lives by the truth comes into
the light, so that it may be seen plainly that what he has
done has been done through God.' When people receive or
reject the Lord Jesus Christ, they are passing judgement
day verdict upon themselves. In preparing people for Jesus
to be revealed to the nation of the Jews, John was preparing
people for judgement day. Those who truly owned up
to their sins would be looking for the Saviour. Those who
went on in the pretence and hypocrisy of being good enough
for God by their 'religion' would reject Jesus. That judgement stands for eternity. 'Through the law and through
"Elijah" ', says Malachi, 'the Lord will graciously seek to
prepare you for the last day.' But he warns them to take
heed.

'Or else I will come and strike the land with a curse'
(4:6). This last phrase of the book is truly staggering. It is
staggering because all through the Old Testament the
promised land had been the centre of the Jewish outlook.
The land was holy. The land was where God dwelt. Now God
was saying, 'Unless you listen to the ministry of John the
Baptist, I am finished with you.' We are reminded that with
the book of Malachi we do stand at the very end of the
Old Testament. Sadly, the Jews generally rejected their
Messiah and the prediction and warning of Malachi came
to pass. The Jews were turned out of the land, soon after
New Testament times, and it is only in this century that

some of them have returned. Because of their transgression and rejection of Jesus, salvation has come to the Gentiles. The door of salvation still stands open for the Jews, but it is only as they turn to their true Messiah that they will be saved. The old religion of sacrifice and of God dwelling in the land of Israel is finished. God warned them, but they generally took no notice.

The lesson from the end of Malachi may be found by pursuing the following line of thinking. God told them to prepare. But what did God give as the sign that if they took notice and began to change they were changing in the right direction? What was the mark that would show that they had received the Lord's words rightly? The answer is the beginning of verse 6. Elijah would come to prepare them and if his ministry were accepted as the Lord intended it should be then, '**He will turn the hearts of the fathers to their children, and the hearts of the children to their fathers.**' At the most basic level, the sign that 'Elijah's' ministry had had the desired effect would be a transformation of heart which results in *love*.

In the New Testament the critical mark that shows that you are properly prepared for judgement day is love. It is love to God, our Father in heaven, and love to others, especially his children. If you have experienced the love of God in eternal salvation, it will make you into a loving person. 'Religion' is of no account. 'For in Christ Jesus neither circumcision nor uncircumcision has any value. The only thing that counts is faith expressing itself through *love*' (Galatians 5:6). The apostle stresses this emphasis in his most famous passage: 'If I speak in the tongues of men and of angels, but have not love, I am only a resounding gong or a clanging cymbal. If I have the gift of prophecy and can fathom all mysteries and all knowledge, and if I have a faith that can move mountains, but have not love, I am nothing. If I give all I possess to the poor and surrender my body to the flames, but have not love, I am nothing' (1 Corinthians 13:1—3).

We are saved by faith in our Lord Jesus Christ. But what is the hallmark of true faith, which distinguishes it from false presumption? True faith expresses itself not just by adherence to biblical doctrine, not just by an outwardly pure life, but by a life of heartfelt service and love. 'God is love. Whoever lives in love lives in God, and God in him' (1 John 4:16). Heaven is indeed a world of love, and only as we learn to love are we being prepared to enter that place. We are only prepared for the day of the Lord as we have faith in Jesus which is shown by practical love.

But Malachi is a true prophet and he does not leave us with just the general principle of love. He applies it to a particular situation.

The generation gap

The background to Malachi's book is the cynical, self-righteous 'faith' of the religious people of his day. By the time of our Lord Jesus Christ, one of the effects of this cynicism was a very negative attitude towards children. After all, they were such a nuisance and made such a noise in the temple courts! Following Jesus' cleansing of the temple we read, 'But when the chief priests and the teachers of the law saw the wonderful things he did and the children shouting in the temple area, "Hosanna to the Son of David," they were indignant' (Matthew 21:15). The children's 'stupidly' simple faith in Jesus did not go down too well with the sophisticated and enlightened religious leaders of the day! The hearts of the fathers and the children were far apart. Yet Jesus often directed his disciples to a child as their example (Mark 9:36,37).

The prophet Malachi applies his principle of a faith which expresses itself by love to the generation gap. When 'Elijah' comes, 'he will turn the hearts of the fathers to their children, and the hearts of the children to their fathers; or else . . .' (4:6). In Christian families and in church fellowships the most blatant lack of love and understanding can often be across the generation gap.

I can remember shopping with my wife in a supermarket and glancing at one of the 'homemaker' magazines which are often available near the check-out. On the front was a headline for an article which read, 'Is there life after kids?' It reflected a prevalent attitude. Children are the death of joy in marriage. Children are a pain in the neck! There may be many reasons for the world to adopt that view. The expense of children, the attention children require disturb the materialistic, easy life-style. Sometimes children are less than sweet little darlings! But that attitude should never become part of the Christian parents' outlook. If it does, changes need to take place in our homes and in our hearts. The Lord is grieved by such things.

Rebellious 'Christian' teenagers who view parents with resentment are not prepared for the Day of Judgement. Unloving 'Christian' parents who make little or no attempt to understand their youngsters and the pressures of the world they live in are unprepared for the Day of Judgement. I am not saying that every Christian family must be perfect. But there *must* be love there, both ways across the generation gap.

Again, a Christian church which is beset by a generation gap within its ranks is hardly pleasing to the Lord. Are there young people in the church who can view the older members with contempt as old 'fuddy-duddies'? Are there young people who can write off the efforts of those who have stood for the truth of the gospel over forty or fifty years as dead and dreary? Then there is something very wrong with those young people. In the last fifteen years or so, Western society has got quite used to evangelical Christians. It is not such a stigma as it was to be branded a 'born-again' Christian. Yet forty or fifty years ago to stand for Christ was far more difficult. It was often to be labelled next to an imbecile to be a Bible-believer. Yet our older friends stood for Christ then. How dare youngsters write off those who bore the heat and burden of the day of fighting for Christ amid the vicious scepticism of the earlier part of the twentieth century?

Are there older people in the churches who reject younger believers because of the way they dress, or whatever? Very often I feel there can almost be a resentment among the older believers that the youngsters have more freedom than they did in their youth. Sometimes an attitude grows up which almost verges on saying, 'We didn't have that freedom when we were young and we are therefore going to make jolly sure you youngsters don't have that freedom.' There can be a jealousy across the generation gap. Young people can be viewed as a disturbance and an irritant to an otherwise peaceful church.

Probably one of the greatest tragedies of the church at the end of the twentieth century is that the generation gap has split churches and continues to divide Christians. Different 'styles' of church are emerging. One is based on youthful music and freedom of worship. One is based on tradition. Very often the great theological debates over formats for worship are nothing but a thin disguise for a lack of love and understanding between the generations. The old are written off as 'dead' and the young are dismissed as 'frothy and shallow'. God hates this division. He longs to see the churches healed. He longs for the hearts of the fathers to be turned to their children and the hearts of the children to be turned to their fathers. He lovingly longs for us all to be prepared for the coming day of the Lord.

Conclusion

Malachi addresses himself to the problem of spiritual degeneration, of living faith deteriorating into empty formalism. It is time to review what answers he has given us. Do we feel that the edge has gone from our spiritual lives? Do we fear that a lack of reality is stealthily creeping into our Christian experience? How much life and affection for Christ is actually there behind the well-worn evangelical clichés we use? If we have to confess that such questions do worry us, Malachi has taught us some valuable lessons and has pointed to the remedy.

The spiritual decline in Israel at the time of Malachi was shown by the priests' acceptance of blemished sacrifices, their irreverence and their perverting the teaching of the law to suit their own ends. Following the lead of the priests, the people had also strayed from the covenant obligations into marriage with people of other religions, marital infidelity, not paying tithes and ungodly talk against the Lord.

The prophet's response to the situation has been a mixture of both encouragement and warning. This is a marvellous and effective mixture. We all enjoy being encouraged and rightly so. But very often our hearts are so hard that we need something a little sterner actually to move us. At the other extreme a diet of nothing but castigation and rebuke for our sins leaves us immobile through feeling totally crushed so that we give up. Malachi understands us very well and so he comes to us with incentives of both kinds.

Primarily Malachi has laid before us the two great rubrics of the biblical message, namely, God's love and God's wrath. God's love is shown in his choice of Israel (1:2), his making with them a covenant of life and peace (2:5), his unchanging

135

commitment to the nation in spite of its sins (3:6) and his delight in his treasured possession of those who fear and honour his name (3:16,17). God's wrath is illustrated by his attitude towards Edom (1:4), his threatening to curse the priests for their irreverence (2:1,2,9), and Malachi's warning of the coming Day of Judgement (4:1).

The spiritual decline within Israel, as indeed at any time among those who profess to be God's people, was constituted of two factors. There were those who sincerely loved the Lord but who had grown careless, and there were those who were God's people in name only and whose religion was insincere and hypocritical. Malachi has presented the facts of God's wrath and God's love to his contemporaries in an attempt to move them to repentance. Being confronted with the goodness and love of God for his soul and the wrath from which he has been saved will always lead a true believer to seek God afresh. Someone who can look upon the love of God and presumptuously go on in his sins only betrays the counterfeit nature of his profession of faith. To the trembling sincere souls who are genuinely grieved over their carelessness and lack of progress in holiness Malachi tenderly gives encouragement with God's unchanging love towards them. But to the arrogant religious hypocrites, who shed no tears over sins, Malachi gives a warning of judgement to come, hoping that they might be brought to true repentance, casting themselves upon God. So the main theme of Malachi is sincerity of heart towards God.

Is our faith becoming formal and unreal? Then we must repent. Have ease and comfort become our gods rather than the Lord? Then by removing his blessing from us God is seeking to wake us up to our folly. ' "Return to me, and I will return to you," says the Lord Almighty' (3:7). The answer to losing touch with God is repentance.

But the primary lesson of Malachi is that repentance is always specific and practical. The commands of Malachi always have to do with concrete issues and definite situations. To leave our repentance in the realm of the general is to leave it in the realm of theory, and that is not to repent at all. Offering of blemished sacrifices had to stop. Mixed religion marriages had to stop. Adulterous thoughts had to stop. Their tithing practices had to change. Their cynical language about God had to cease and be replaced by the language of faith. Repentance meant concrete changes born of the fear and love of God.

Are you in that spiritual state in which vital faith seems to be waning? Do you seem to have lost contact with God? Then the message of Malachi is that you will not find him again by leaving repentance in the realm of sentiment or theory. There must be specific, practical repentance.

If, as you have read Scripture, the Holy Spirit has been convicting you about the fact that so much of your outlook and goals in life are in fact those of the world, with a thin veneer of 'Christianity' on top, then you will not renew living fellowship with God simply through a vague acknowledgement of the situation. There must be sorrow over how you have let God down, leading to a practical change in how you live your life. Is the situation that we do love God, but we are ashamed over the meagreness of our love? Then although an acknowledgement of that fact before God in prayer is good, we dare not leave it there. We must seek to fire our hearts by viewing the greatness of God in Scripture and must plead with the Lord to give us a greater measure of the Holy Spirit that we might have something of the heartfelt affection towards him which he desires and deserves.

Perhaps that practical change will mean a loss of face in the eyes of others. Perhaps it will mean a diet of having to swallow your pride and eat your words! But it is utterly foolish to let such things stand in your way. You must repent and return to God. What is more important, your standing in the eyes of men or your standing in the eyes of God?

Perhaps for someone reading this book, God has been putting his finger on a certain area of your life and it would be best for you to stop reading now and break your heart before God now and confess your sin and think out, God helping you, practical ways in which to effect change. 'Return to me, and I will return to you,' said God (3:7).

'How are we to return?' said the people (3:7). For Malachi's contemporaries it was in the very practical area of tithing. And God is calling us to practical repentance.

Malachi lays before his people every encouragement to turn to God afresh. As they repent and start living as they should, the surrounding nations will begin to see something of God in them and Israel will begin to fulfil that purpose of being a light to the Gentiles for which God chose them (1:11; 3:12). As they hear God's rebukes for their sins and his calls to repentance, they should see in them God's gracious purpose of seeking to refine them and do them good (3:2). The worst thing in the world is not when God rebukes us, but when he stops speaking to us and leaves us to our own devices. Malachi encourages them by his assertion from God that sincere obedience will lead to God's pouring out his blessing upon them. To those who whole-heartedly seek God, he will 'throw open the floodgates of heaven and pour out so much blessing that you will not have room enough for it' (3:11). He encourages his people further to renew their obedience by his description of those who, with all their failings, nevertheless respond to God's Word sincerely. He calls them God's sons and God's treasured possession (3:17). Such people can have assurance in the face of the coming day of the Lord (4:2).

This prophecy of Malachi is extremely pertinent to our times. When Jesus ascended into heaven he left just a few hundred disciples in the world. Yet within one generation those people could be said to have 'turned the world upside down' for Christ. Today there are literally thousands, perhaps millions, of people in Britain and America who attend Bible-preaching churches, and yet the effect we have upon the moral and spiritual climate of our nations is literally pathetic. Could it be that far too many of those church-attenders, for all their profession, are in fact in the state described in this book? They have lost touch with the living God. ' "Return to me, and I will return to you," says the Lord Almighty.'

Notes

1. Allan Ahlberg, *Please Mrs Butler*, Penguin Books, p. 38.
2. C. H. Spurgeon, *Flashes of Thought*, Passmore & Alabaster, p. 260.
3. Jock Andersen, *Worship the Lord*, IVP, pp. 17–18.
4. Quoted in *Five Pioneer Missionaries*, Banner of Truth Trust, pp. 24–25.
5. Poems of Prevert, Penguin Books, p. 69.
6. Quoted in Arnold Dallimore, *George Whitefield Vol. 1*, Banner of Truth Trust, p. 152.
7. J. C. Ryle, *Christian Leaders*, Chas. J. Thynne, pp. 272–3.
8. Alan Stibbs, *God's Church*, IVP, p. 7.
9. Churches founded upon the biblical gospel share a common faith, which can find expression in a simple doctrinal statement, like say, the doctrinal basis of the UCCF. This sets out belief in:
   a. The unity of the Father, the Son and the Holy Spirit in the Godhead.
   b. The sovereignty of God in creation, revelation, redemption and final judgement.
   c. The divine inspiration and infallibility of Holy Scripture as originally given, and its supreme authority in all matters of faith and conduct.
   d. The universal sinfulness and guilt of human nature since the Fall, rendering man subject to God's wrath and condemnation.
   e. Redemption from the guilt, penalty and power of sin only through the sacrificial death (as our Representative and Substitute) of Jesus Christ, the incarnate Son of God.
   f. The resurrection of Jesus Christ from the dead.
   g. The necessity of the work of the Holy Spirit to make the death of Christ effective to the individual sinner, granting him repentance towards God and faith in Jesus Christ.
   h. The indwelling and work of the Holy Spirit within the believer.
   i. The one holy universal church, which is the body of Christ and to which all true believers belong.
   j. The expectation of the personal return of the Lord Jesus Christ.
10. P. R. Reid, *The Colditz Story*, Pan Books, pp. 149, 150.
11. Life of Robert Flockhart, BBH, p. 144.
12. Al Martin, *Banner of Truth* Magazine, Issue 106–107, 1972, pp. 23, 24.
13. Roland Bainton, *Here I Stand*, Mentor Books, p. 235.
14. Daniel Defoe, *Robinson Crusoe*, Penguin Edition, p. 38.
15. Harold Faber, *Book of Laws*, Sphere Books.

16. C. H. Spurgeon, *An All-round Ministry*, Banner of Truth Trust, p. 3.
17. *Book of Laws.*
18. John Angell James, *The Young Man from Home*, old edition, p. 98.

For further reading on Malachi:
Joyce Baldwin, *Haggai, Zechariah and Malachi* (Tyndale Commentary), IVP.
T. V. Moore, *Haggai and Malachi*, Banner of Truth Trust.